Sponsored by

The Playboater's Handbook

The Reference for Freestyle Kayaking Technique

by World Rodeo Champion
Ken Whiting

With foreword by Bob McDonough, and feature articles on choosing the right playboat and paddle

Photos by Tina Mohns

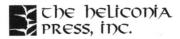

The Heliconia Press, Inc.

The Playboater's Handbook - The Reference for Freestyle
    Kayaking Technique.
Copyright © 1998 by Ken Whiting. All rights reserved
ISBN 1-896980-02-3

All descriptions, illustrations, and layout by Ken Whiting unless
otherwise noted.

All photos by Tina Mohns unless otherwise noted.

Front Cover: Ken Whiting at McKoy's on the Ottawa River.
Photo by Tina Mohns.
Back Cover: Ken Whiting in Horseshoe Hole on the Ottawa River.
Photo by Tina Mohns.

Printed and bound in Canada

The Heliconia Press
PO Box 200
Clayton, Ontario
Canada
K0A 1P0
613-256-7300

This book is dedicated to my parents, who opened their minds and hearts to the hedonistic, paddling lifestyle that has guided me since my early high school days.

———————————

Contents

Acknowledgements

*A*s this project comes to an end, I look back and realize how heavily dependent I have been on the help of friends and family. Without their contributions of time, energy and patience, I know my goals would not have been met. A sincere and special thank you goes to my parents, Bill and Diane, who unceasingly provided their support, guidance, and brain power to help see the project finished in this millennium. I owe my unending gratitude to Nicole Zaharko, who has put up with so much over the past year while encouraging and supporting me in the different paths I have taken. I thank my brother, Jeff, who also provided unlimited support and guidance, and who allowed me to learn from his trials and errors! My deepest thanks go to Bob McDonough for his huge contribution of time in providing invaluable feedback, and to Tina Mohns who also contributed her time and great talents, while making our many photo shoots a pleasure.

A final thank you goes to all those who have provided their support in one way or another to see this project through. I thank the lads and lasses of the Ottawa for keeping my passion for paddling alive all these years, as well as Claudia and Dirk Van Wijk for believing in me when I was younger and longer-haired. Thanks to my grandmother, Phyllis, who has somehow kept her faith in me. Cheers go to Jim Hargreaves, Steve Zarnowski, Lynn Clark, Lee Gagne, and all the advertisers whose faith and support were so crucial for this project's success.

About the Author

*A*t the age of 14, in the summer of 1989, Ken Whiting experienced whitewater for the first time while taking a 5-day kayaking course on the Ottawa River. The summer of 1990 found Ken supporting his newly-found and immediate addiction to kayaking, by working with a rafting company on the Ottawa. His love for the sport postponed academic plans as he sought to quiet the hedonist within. Consequently, Ken's paddling has taken him to all corners of North America as well as throughout Europe, Japan, Australia, Honduras and Guatemala. Through these travels he managed a number of first descents in Honduras and Canada, and has been the featured paddler in a number of videos ranging from 'Kayaks and Coconuts' (a Central American paddling adventure), to 'Walls of Freedom' and 'Breathe' (extreme skiing and kayaking films). In 1994 Ken's competitiveness broke through the surface as he began frequenting whitewater rodeos across the continent. Since that time, Ken has won a number of major rodeos culminating in his ultimate success in the fall of 1997 when he became the World Whitewater Rodeo Kayaking Champion. This Playboater's Handbook marks the beginning of Ken's publishing career and was written and assembled on the same Ottawa River banks that enticed him 9 years ago.

Introduction

I can still vividly remember that sunny day in July 1995, sitting on the banks of the Eiskenal in Augsburg, Germany, watching in fascination as my paddling heroes (those I'd seen on videos or heard surreal tales about) danced about in the Washing Machine hole. As a Canadian, I had always been somewhat isolated from the rodeo scene and was forced to learn everything from scratch. I spent hours that day watching Bob, Mark, Clay, Bernd, Ollie, Jan, and so many others, analysing their every move. Later that afternoon I put my newly-found knowledge to the test and was astounded by the results. Since then, I've been lucky enough to spend significant time on the river banks learning from those same paddlers-an opportunity I greatly credit for my paddling successes.

Rodeo (freestyle paddling) is developing at an incredible rate these days. Equipment changes make the once unthinkable now possible, while increased participation drives the level of competition to new heights, and finds paddlers pushing their limits further each day. More importantly, the advances being made with equipment have made it easier for both current, and aspiring paddlers alike, to experience the joy of whitewater.

This book was conceived to enhance the experience of the ever-growing number of playboaters on today's rivers. Though no book can compare to actual river experiences, what I've attempted to provide is a base from which the various freestyle moves can be visualized. After all, how can you expect to perform a move you've only dreamed of doing, if you don't know how the dream should appear! To provide this understanding, each skill has been broken down into a few basic concepts, then further analysed in more depth. It is my hope that this will enable paddlers of all skill levels to benefit.

So, where does kayaking go from here? Will freestyle kayaking continue to grow in popularity, and amaze us with its further developments? Only time will tell! Regardless, the kayak will always be a major link between human and whitewater. It is my simple yet sincere hope that as the sport grows in popularity, the new people getting involved will be as caring and concerned about the land that we play in, as the majority of today's paddlers are.

Playboating! It's a good sign when you want to take up a sport with a name beginning with 'play'. Gone are the days when the advancement in your whitewater skills was measured solely by the difficulty of the rivers you'd paddled. Now, it's just as common to measure your paddling skills by the degree to which your freestyle skills are honed. The top boaters of the past were those who conquered their fears and mastered their skills in order to run the most difficult and dangerous rivers. Today's top freestyle boaters can master their freestyle skills without the fear element. The elimination of the fear element and the fact that the sport is so much fun are the reasons the sport of playboating is booming today.

Back when I started my freestyle career in the mid-80s, the tricks to master, in the big-surface boats, were 360s and pirouettes. With so few tricks, you pulled anything out of your hat to impress the judges in the freestyle competitions. The learning curve for freestyle moves peaked quickly and only the diehard competitive paddlers perfected those skills to an extreme.

The limits of what was possible in a kayak expanded greatly as squirt-boating became popular in the mid-80s. Squirt-boating was the first really technical whitewater freestyle sport. The moves that were developed in squirt-boats are closely related to the playboating moves done in the plastic freestyle boats of today. Many of today's freestyle boaters hone their skills in squirt-boats.

Today, if you go to your local river's freestyle rapids, you'll find the local quiver of talent waiting in line for their next ride and a new chance to show off their talents or to practice a new move. It's pretty much the same at snowboarding parks where there's a crowd of boarders waiting in line for their turn at the best jumps. I dread wipe-outs on my snowboard, but in

11

playboating, when you learn good, safe technique, the biggest wipe-outs end with a simple roll and a calm paddle back up the eddy to get in line once again. It never crosses my mind to fear the wipe-out.

The aim of this book is to get the knowledge of how freestyle tricks are performed into the minds of the paddlers in order to increase everyone's skills and everyone's fun. If you understand how the freestyle tricks are performed, what's happening to your kayak, and what's going on in the rapids during these moves, this book will have succeeded in helping you to master many of the moves that may, at this point, seem unattainable.

As you begin to understand what's happening to your body, your boat, and in the rapid during these freestyle tricks, you'll begin to imagine or visualize yourself doing these moves. This basic awareness of how these maneuvers are performed is the beginning of being able to master them yourself. This book, along with watching the local hotshot paddlers and good technique on video, will help you on your way to mastering the moves in your own boat, on your own river.

———————

13

What You Need For The Hottest Moves

*A*nyone can perform any of the play moves listed in this book. These moves aren't only for the elite paddlers. They have just learned them first. As long as you have the desire to learn, can visualize the moves and have the time to practice them, you're already well on your way.

There are a few other key ingredients to enhance your learning curve. It is important to approach the rivers with respect, understanding that we aren't attempting to control the water's power, but to play with it. At the same time, an aggressive 'Go get 'em' attitude will go a long way in helping you learn, as long as you stay within your capabilities. Dropping into holes and surfing waves can be a very intimidating experience. One of the best ways to shed some of your hesitancy is to get comfortable with your 'Eskimo roll' as you're guaranteed to spend plenty of time upside-down while learning the moves.

It's also a good idea to start slowly each day and gradually move to the harder play moves as your body loosens up. Playboating is a high-impact activity. If you haven't given your body time to warm up, you could very easily injure yourself. Start your day on land with a stretching program. Once on the water, spend some time warming up those crucial paddling muscles with some flatwater paddling exercises. When you're ready to move on, start with some stern squirting, front surfing, or other moves that won't take every ounce of your strength.

Finally, the equipment you use will also dictate the ease with which many of the play moves can be executed. Though many of these moves were developed a number of years ago, the newer boats and gear have been designed to make them easier to do. Bob McDonough's article on choosing the right kayak will let you know what to look for in a playboat that will best suit your needs.

Using this Book

*T*his book was written with the knowledge that I've attained over 9 years of dedicated playboating. These are the techniques that I've found to work, and that I've watched many other paddlers put into action. They were developed by our body's responding to our actions until the most efficient method was realized. This book should provide an understanding of some key concepts that can enable you to skip a good chunk of the learning path. With these concepts in mind, it will then be up to you to hit the rivers and practice, as no book can compare with the real experiences had on a river. Even still, what we visualize doing is not always the reality of our actions. Quality instruction can help advance your paddling to the next level both in skills and in safety.

The Ins and Outs of Playboating

What's up with all these new designs? The competition between the manufacturing companies is heating up, the state-of-the-art freestyle kayak is evolving rapidly, and the paddlers are reaping the rewards with kayaks that perform the freestyle moves more easily than ever before.

So how do you decide which freestyle kayak is the best one for you? In choosing a new design weigh the following criteria:

Effort Needed to Tilt the Kayak on Edge

When you're in the water, can you easily tilt the kayak up on edge? When you're setting up for cartwheels or carving turns, your kayak needs to be held on edge with a steady tilt. A kayak that tilts easily will let you play much longer than one which requires a lot of effort to get up on edge and stay there.

In general, the wider and flatter the hull of a kayak, the more difficult it will be to hold a steady boat tilt. This means that the conventional, round-hulled kayaks, are somewhat easier to control (boat tilts will be steadier and easier, while your transition between tilts will be smoother). On the other hand, these round-hulled boats are a bit more limiting in their play potential, as flat spinning is not possible. You must decide what is of most importance to you.

Something to consider: A lighter paddler will have more difficulty tilting a flat-hulled kayak on its edge. On the other hand, a lighter paddler displaces less water when sitting in his or her kayak, meaning that the kayak will plane more easily than if a heavier paddler were using it. What this means, is that if a kayak requires too much effort for a lighter person to tilt, a narrower kayak, with a hull that may not be quite as flat, will make tilting easier, without necessarily losing the planing capabilities. Inversely, a heavier paddler will have less trouble tilting a flat-hulled kayak on edge, and will need a wider, flatter, surface area on the hull to help the kayak plane more easily. A good design should plane well and allow you to easily tilt the kayak on edge. A kayak with some type of bevelled edge on the hull will help in both of these areas.

Comfort

Don't skimp here. Finding a kayak that best fits your body should be one of your main goals. Are you comfortable? Does it enhance your ability to maintain an aggressive body position? Good posture is critical for getting the most out of the power in your upper body (your torso's rotation). Bad posture can inhibit your ability to perform the moves, while contributing to those stresses that lead to back pain. Are your legs high enough so that you can really crank your knees sideways when trying to swing your ends into those cartwheels? Does the sitting position put any strain on your ankles?

When trying out different kayaks, the position of your knees in the thigh hooks tends to make the biggest difference with regard to comfort. What is a comfortable position for one person, may be agonizing for another. This is dependent on both your leg size, and your flexibility. A kayak with a lower front deck will usually be more comfortable for a shorter, or more flexible paddler. A taller, less flexible person may find that sitting up straight in this kayak is a constant strain, while leaning the body all the way forward is downright impossible. Inversely, a kayak with a higher front deck may leave shorter paddlers struggling for control over the kayak's great bulk.

The position of your feet will also have a large bearing on your comfort in a kayak. Many of the newer kayaks have had large amounts of volume removed from the ends, to allow them to slice through the water with less resistance. This works great to facilitate cartwheels and the like, but can put taller paddlers in an awkward foot position. If your feet are forced into an unnatural position (not kept in line with the rest of your leg) then your knees and ankles will usually pay the price.

The key to choosing a kayak that you will be happy with, is finding one that provides a favourable "fun to pain" ratio. For most people, a kayak can be found that is both comfortable, and more than adequately responsive. There are those people out there who are willing to sacrifice comfort in a kayak for an added bit of responsiveness. If this is you, make sure that the discomfort doesn't outweigh the fun you're having. There is no surer way to tire of a sport, than to associate that sport with constant pain.

Flat spinning

Does it plane easily when on a good wave? Once planing, does it spin easily from the bow to the stern and just as easily from the stern to the bow. There are a lot of new designs available now that don't reach a full plane or flat spin adequately. So, test the designs out and quiz the best boaters to find out how a particular model is performing.

In general, the wider, and the longer the flat area on a hull, the more apt the kayak will be to plane and to spin. The reason for this is that the body's weight is distributed over a greater area. With this in mind, it is safe to say that a lighter paddler will be able to get away with a slightly smaller planing surface, while still having great spinning potential.

Cartwheeling

Can you engage both ends with ease in a hole or in a pourover? One test for this is your ability to get the ends underwater in flatwater (see 'Winding Up the Bow' in the cartwheel segment). Getting the bow several inches underwater on flatwater is about the same as what you'll need to accomplish initiating the bow when in a hole. (Don't expect to be able to throw your ends down in flatwater right away. Read the

'Winding Up the Bow' segment, and practice rocking your stern and bow alternately into the air. This drill takes practice and can be difficult even with a very small kayak.

The thinner the ends of a kayak are, the more easily they will slice down, through the water. Bigger paddlers may need more foot room, resulting in the choice of a kayak with bigger volume ends. Though these kayaks will be less apt to slice through the water, the larger paddler's added weight will usually compensate for this. On the other hand, a smaller paddler's feet lie closer to the center of the kayak where there is ample foot room. Added volume in the ends of the kayak might be helpful when running rivers, but won't help for most playboating manoeuvres.

———————

Without a doubt, the kayak is your biggest whitewater investment. With so many new models now available, and so many more on the way, it's worth taking the time to test a number of them and to quiz the hottest paddlers in your area. The good news is that after extensive testing I have found that all recent designs perform incredibly well. Of course, each kayak has its strengths and weaknesses, but as long as you choose your kayak with the clear understanding of what is most important to you, I'm confident that you will not be disappointed.

Ken

Paddle Talk

Paddles are very personal pieces of equipment. There is no one paddle type that is best for all kayakers, but there are some things to think about before choosing a paddle for yourself.

Ideally, you will be holding your paddle with a wide enough grip so that your arms are bent at 90 degrees at the elbows. Sliding your hands closer together may feel more comfortable in the beginning, but won't provide you with the same power or control. Most playboaters prefer a shorter paddle to the one they might use on a normal river-running day as it is quicker and easier to move around both above and below the water surface.

With arms bent at 90 degrees at the elbows, there are only a couple of inches between hand and blade. This gives great control for quick and precise strokes, but you'll get less leverage from the blades.

With arms bent at 90 degrees at the elbows, many playboaters will have only 2 - 4 inches between their hands and the actual paddle blades. Holding your paddle this close to the blades has its pros and cons. The drawback is a decrease in leverage that you receive. This makes for less effective braces, and slightly more difficult rolls. You also won't achieve quite as much power from your strokes as you would with a longer paddle. On the other hand, the increased manoeuvrability you get from a shorter paddle is undeniable. Try lifting a paddle's blade by picking the paddle up at the opposite end. This is not easy to do! The closer you grab the paddle to the blade you're trying to lift, the easier it gets, and the more control you have.

Holding the paddle fairly close to the blades adds speed and precision to your strokes.

Understanding your possible hand positions on the paddle, it's now time to consider how you will grip the shaft. Hold the paddle firmly in your control hand, yet not so hard that your knuckles turn white! For most people, the control hand will be their right. Let the shaft move freely in the other hand. Playboating involves an inordinate amount of turning, bracing and rolling, which might cause your hands to wander around the shaft. Placing some type of index that enables you to confirm your hands' positions without having to look down, will make life easier on you.

The best way to get more playboating performance out of your paddle, while at the same time appeasing your aching wrists, is to use a paddle with a small degree of blade off-set. It is most common for playboaters to use blades that are off-set at around 45 degrees. This cuts down on the movement your control wrist needs to do, while also letting you use both blades simultaneously for control in some situations. If you are paddling with blades off-set under 45 degrees, that's great too, (I use a 30 degree paddle) but you'd better hope you aren't paddling upwind all day!

When vertical, you'll sometimes find both your blades in the water. Using a paddle with less twist enables both these blades to brace, or work effectively at the same time.

The paddle you choose should be determined by the type of boating you do. Paddling shouldn't be a pain. If it feels good, stick with it! If your wrists do hurt, relax your grip on the paddle. If that doesn't help, then think of getting a paddle with less twist. If it's your shoulder that's bothering you, try a paddle with smaller blades. A large blade can put an enormous stress on the body when it catches water.

Sit up Straight! Relax...

*T*o my knowledge, they have yet to develop the 'La-z-boy' kayak! Until they do, there is no excuse for paddling with bad posture. Quit slouching!

Sitting up straight and leaning forward slightly at the hips puts a paddler in both a stable and aggressive position. You'll be amazed at how much more control and power this can provide.

Just because you're sitting a bit straighter than you might normally, you needn't be all tight and stiff. Relax! Let your upper and lower bodies move independently, yet co-operatively. Whitewater isn't totally predictable, so allow your lower body the freedom to 'go with the flow' while keeping your upper body balanced over the kayak.

This looseness at the hips will also increase the amount of boat tilt you can achieve. A strong and confident boat tilt is vital in all facets of paddling. When tilting your kayak up on edge, balance your weight on a single butt cheek, steadying yourself with your upper knee. A sure way of staying balanced like this, is by keeping your head over your kayak.

Finding a boat that fits both your body, and your needs, will enhance your ability to sit up straight, rotate your torso, and utilize the power of your whole upper body while paddling. See the section `Choosing the Right Playboat for You` for more information on what to look for.

Whatever you might be doing, remember: where your head leads, your body will follow. So use judgement as to where you let your head lead you. When tilting your kayak on edge, keep your head over your kayak.

— *A head that stays over the kayak's edge helps ensure a balanced position by keeping all weight off the paddle, and on the kayak instead.*

— *As your head falls to one side, your body follows. This keeps your paddle hard at work bracing, and unable to perform other jobs.*

Torso Rotation

Why does a baseball pitcher go through a wind-up? He does it because he can't harness nearly as much power from using his arm alone to throw. The same goes for kayaking, though the wind-up isn't quite as obvious!

Torso rotation (or shoulder rotation) is the most effective method of getting the most muscle involved in each and every stroke. This co-operative motion is the base from which all play manoeuvres stem.

So, how exactly does one successfully use the torso rotation to one's advantage? Firstly, it must be understood that you want to use your whole upper body to pull the kayak in the

This is how much the upper body is winding up for a regular forward stroke. The whole upper body turns, and the front shoulder pushes forward in order to reach the paddle to the toes.

As the stroke takes place, the upper body is brought back square with the legs (effectively unwinding the body) and your other shoulder punches forward, winding-up for your next stroke.

desired direction. Consider your paddle planting in the water as a pivot from which you can pull your kayak past, rather than a stroke that pulls your blade through the water. Having planted your paddle, your strokes should be taken with an attempt to keep your shoulders in line with your paddle shaft. This will cause your shoulders to turn with each stroke, using more of your bigger muscles (stomach, back, pecs...) to pull on the blade, while using your arms less.

*W*inding up your body when paddling refers to turning your upper body so that the line between your shoulders is no longer square with the direction that your kayak points. By planting your paddle with your upper body wound up, you can

————Sweep stroke finishes with shoulders turned in an attempt to stay parallel to the paddle. Notice the torso is turned enough to view the whole front of the lifejacket.

use your stomach muscles to pull your legs back to their position of rest, while you push or pull on the paddle, using your arms, chest and back muscles. This co-operative motion between stomach and upper torso muscles, pulling your body back to its position of rest, will be referred to as *unwinding*.

Every stroke taken, whether it be a small correction stroke, a forward stroke, a sweep or even a rudder, should use the strength of your stomach, chest and back muscles as well as your arms.

T𝕙e Braces

Without having developed a safe and effective brace, a few days of playing in the whitewater will probably leave your hips sore, and your sinuses full. On any river, doing any type of paddling, the brace can either be your best friend or your worst enemy. If done correctly, you'll spend less and less time underwater. If done incorrectly, you could become the next victim of a shoulder injury.

Unfortunately, a shoulder dislocation is one of the most common paddling injuries. By keeping your arms low, never fully extending them, and following the rules of the braces, you will help keep your shoulders strong and healthy.

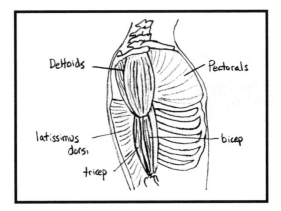

The shoulder has a wider range of motion than any other joint and is controlled by a number of large muscle groups in the back, chest and arms. These are important muscles to strengthen and stretch to keep your shoulders healthy.

There are two types of braces you will find useful: the low brace, and the high brace. For both, it is important to understand that the function of the brace is not to push boat and body back to the upright position, but rather to stop your flipping momentum and to provide a platform that will allow your hips and knees to do the rest.

The Low Brace

The low brace is a safe brace to use as your arms act like shock-absorbers. The position for a low brace requires your forearms to be rotated down with your elbows held above the paddle. You now have your shocks! From this position, you will be using the back of your blades against the water. Bring your outside elbow in close against your side and reach out at a right angle to your kayak with the blade that will be bracing. The further you reach to the side, the more leverage your brace will achieve, yet the less effective your arm shocks will be. Just remember not to fully extend your arms!

As you begin to flip over, slap the water with the back of your paddle in the low brace position. This should momentarily stall your flip, and provide enough opportunity for your hips and knees to pull the boat upright.

Reaching out at 90 degrees, stop the flip by slapping the water with the back of the blade.

Rotate the boat upright using hips and knees. Sweep the paddle towards the front of the kayak with a sculling angle that forces the blade to the surface.

The last thing to return to its original position is the head, while the paddle breaks free of the water at the toes, ready for a stroke.

If you find your blades diving underwater when bracing, after slapping the water, try sweeping forward with a sculling angle that will slice the blade to the surface.

———————

The High Brace

The high brace is more effective than the low brace, and therefore will often be the first choice for paddlers. If it is done properly, and within a safe range of motion, great, although it does have more potential for slipping into a dangerous position.

A high brace is performed with the elbows below the paddle. To do this, roll your wrists and forearms upwards so that the power face of your paddle is facing down, towards the water. Tuck your outside elbow in close to your side while your inside arm reaches out at 90 degrees to your kayak. Keep everything compact, giving yourself as much room for corrections as possible.

— *Without fully extending, arms reach out, 90 degrees to the kayak, and slap the water to stop the flip. Notice the right elbow kept in close to the body.*

— *Rotate the kayak upright with hips and knees, while keeping the head down.*

— *With boat and body upright, the head is ready to move back over the top of the kayak.*

31

As you begin to flip, reach out to the side of the kayak without fully extending your arm, and slap the water to briefly stop yourself. Leave the remainder of the recovery to your hips and knees, as they rotate the boat back upright. There's a good chance you'll find your paddle diving deeply underwater when performing this brace. If so, try sweeping your brace to the stern, using a sculling angle to bring the blade to the water surface. By sweeping your body to the stern with the paddle, you'll also lower your center of gravity, making your kayak roll more easily. Be sure to get your weight forward immediately afterwards though, or you might soon be repeating the whole process!

The sculling motion that, when performed underwater, will help your blade resurface while still providing bracing power.

When we watch slalom racers and freestyle boaters, we can get an idea of the potential extreme ranges of motion when one strengthens the muscles controlling the shoulder. Keep in mind that these athletes manoeuvrability is at the peak of possible motion due to intense training and strengthening of the joint. Stay compact!

The Clock

*T*hroughout this book I have referred to boat angles in terms of the hours on a clock. The idea behind this is quite simple. The direction from which the current approaches is considered 12 o'clock.

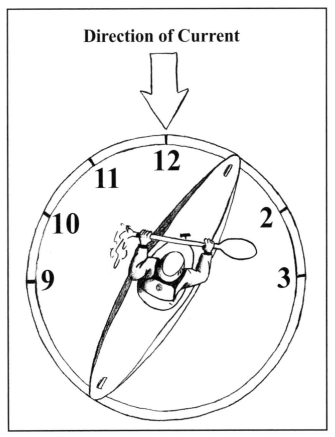

Direction of Current

This paddler has set up with a 1 o'clock angle.

Keep in mind that the clock refers to the current that is affecting the paddler. This current could be at a different angle from that of the main current.

Standing Waves

Standing waves come in all shapes and sizes, with no two being exactly the same. They do share some common characteristics though, and throughout this book they will be referred to by the names in the diagram below.

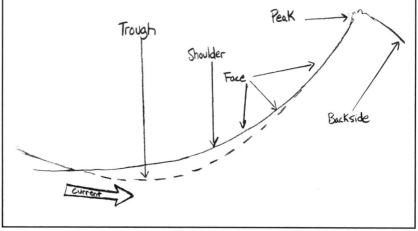

Wave anatomy

As simple as the standing wave seems, there are a few features that must be understood to use it to its full potential. The most important issue to consider is the way in which gravity and the current's speed will act on the kayak at different points on the wave.

Gravity is the driving force behind all types of surfing on standing waves. For surfing to be possible, the force of gravity pulling you down the face of the wave must exceed those forces attempting to pull you downstream (such as the friction of the current on your kayak). This force of gravity will be stronger on steeper waves. Similarly, gravity will be stronger on the steeper *parts* of a wave. Since a wave steepens towards its peak, the closer to the peak one surfs, the more gravity will have an effect.

It is also reasonable to say that the faster the current is moving, the more gravity will be required to keep a surfer from being forced over the peak of the wave, and downstream. It is a commonly overlooked fact that the current's speed is not constant at all points on a wave. Consider the following diagram.

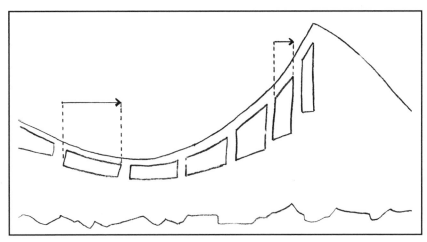

The boxes in the water represent the movement of 1 cubic foot of water in 1 second. The arrows clearly show that the water is slower moving towards the peak of the wave. The fastest moving water is that water rushing downwards towards the trough of the wave.

Combining your understanding that the current's speed is quickest as the water rushes downwards into a wave's trough, with the fact that the force of gravity keeping a surfer on a wave is strongest towards the peak of a wave, it should be easier to visualize spending your surf time on the face of a wave, rather than in the trough. Both wave features are helping to maintain your surf at this point.

Holes

*H*oles can provide the best playspots on a river, but at the same time a hole can be your mother's worst nightmare. Like waves, they are found in all sorts of shapes, with no two being quite alike. Some are great for surfing while others are best avoided like the plague. Being able to differentiate between a friendly hole and a mean hole is really quite simple, and like all skills, gets easier with practice.

Hole Anatomy

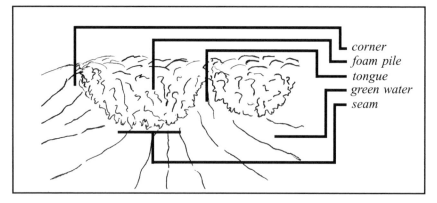

corner
foam pile
tongue
green water
seam

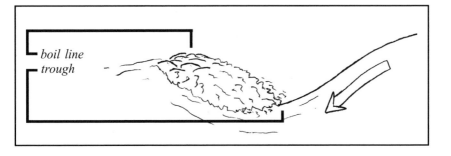

boil line
trough

Choosing a friendly hole

When choosing a friendly hole to surf, you must consider three things. Is it an easy hole to balance in? Is it an easy hole to exit? Is it a safe hole?

The easiest holes to side surf are those holes whose troughs are flat, or almost level. These holes take little energy to side surf since a very slight boat tilt is needed to prevent the upstream edge from catching. Holes in which the green water

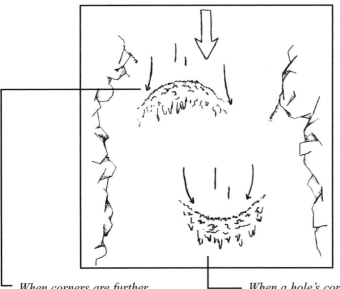

When corners are further downstream than the trough, the water tends to push a paddler out of the hole.

When a hole's corners are upstream of the trough, exiting may be tricky.

flows into the trough at a steep angle are referred to as pour-overs. To surf these holes, one needs a radical boat tilt which usually results in a lot of bracing.

When deciding whether or not a hole will be easy to exit, there is really only one thing to look for. Are the corners of the hole further downstream than its trough? If they are, then the water will naturally push the paddler towards them and make exiting much easier. If the corners are even with, or upstream of the trough, you might want to watch someone go first!

The last issue to take note of when scouting a hole is the safety cushion it provides. Unless you are incredibly sure of your ability to stay upright and to get out of the hole, then choose a hole in which a surprise upstream flip won't send you hurtling into rock. It's also generally a good idea to avoid holes that have a boil line more than a boat length downstream of the seam. These holes have the potential to hold a boat or swimming paddler.

_____

The Moves

Front Surfing

Using gravity to maintain an upstream-facing position on the face of a standing wave.

For many, there is nothing more enjoyable than sitting peacefully on a wave , hypnotized by the water rushing by. Others are only satisfied by front surfing the faster, surging waves, while spray kicks up wildly and the hull of the kayak ripples beneath. Whatever your fancy, front surfing is something that anyone able to confidently cross an eddyline can do.

Getting Established on a Wave

There are two ways of catching a wave: the drop-on technique, or ferrying out from an abutting eddy. The fate of your surf is dependent on your boat angle, speed and placement at the time of entry. So, take your time setting up the right approach.

The Drop-on Technique

This technique involves catching a wave by drifting downstream onto it with your kayak facing upstream. The toughest part of doing this is lining yourself up to hit the steepest part of the wave. Approaching with a ferry angle, and looking over the shoulder that allows the best view of the wave will facilitate this. As you near the wave, slow yourself down as much as possible with some powerful forward strokes. Once

Slow down any downstream momentum with some powerful forward paddling.

Approach the wave on a ferry, looking over the downstream shoulder.

Leaning back when the wave is reached helps keep the bow from purling underwater.

Once the bow is clear of the trough, an aggressive forward lean will help ensure the kayak's position on the face of the wave.

you hit the wave, leaning back will help to lift your bow and prevent it from diving underwater. Keeping the ferry angle that was used for your approach will also help to keep your bow from purling underwater. Once your bow is clear of the wave's trough, you may need to lean forward aggressively to ensure that you don't slide off the backside of the wave.

Side Slipping from an Eddy

Side slipping (ferrying) onto a wave from an abutting eddy is by far the most reliable method of catching a wave since you start with no downstream momentum. Your boat angle, speed and placement are of the utmost importance now that you need to cross an eddy line and maintain a ferry angle. Start as close to the eddy line as possible since you're going to need a strong upstream angle.

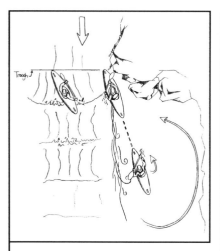

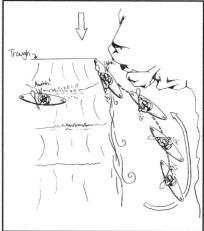

The current in an eddy gets stronger further from the eddy line. Starting an approach close to the eddy line will provide ample time to establish an angle,and make a strong ferry angle easier to achieve.

By starting an approach far from the eddy line, entry angles will need constant adjustment as the kayak gets swept up the eddy.

Next, you'll have to decide where to exit the eddy, and with how much speed and angle. The speed of the main current will help you decide your boat angle and speed. The faster the water is moving, the more speed and upstream angle you'll need. Count on needing an angle fairly close to 12 o'clock. When deciding where to exit the eddy, it is important to understand what part of the wave is best to catch. Try to slip onto the wave, staying on its face the whole time. The water is slower moving here and gravity is also helping to keep you where you

— Crossing the eddy line, the bow should enter the current at, or downstream of, the wave's trough. Ferry onto the wave, staying on its face.

Trough

want to be. Entering too far upstream will land you in the fastest moving water as it rushes downhill towards the wave. This can result in your bow purling or you might end up with enough downstream momentum to carry you up and over the wave.

Surf's Up... What now?

I've caught the wave! It's smooth sailing from here on in, isn't it? Then why am I fighting so hard to stay on the wave?

The first thing that must be understood is that all your surf time is ideally spent on the face of the wave. Keep in mind that the closer to the peak you are, the slower the water is moving and the steeper the wave is. This is all good news for the surfer! Surfing in the trough makes the kayak much less manoeuvrable, and there's also a good chance that your bow will purl.

— For maximum manoeuvrability, surf on the face of the wave.

43

As for your body position, stay relaxed and maintain a good posture while surfing. Leaning back a bit will help to keep your bow from purling, but don't lie too far back as you'll lose an incredible amount of boat control, plus you'll be a lot more unstable. Don't be afraid to change your body lean on a wave either. It's a great way to keep your position on the face of the wave. In general, if you are too close to the trough, leaning back will help pull you backwards, whereas if you are precariously close to the peak, an aggressive forward lean will help you stay on the wave.

Leaning back when in the trough helps prevent the bow from purling, while also helping draw the kayak downstream, onto the face of the wave.

Leaning forward helps move the kayak upstream, down the face of the wave

The final skill you need to master is carving back and forth across the wave to stay on its face. The only way to do this effectively is with both a good rudder and boat tilt.

When ruddering, your paddle should be almost parallel to the direction of your kayak. This means you should be able to drop your paddle from the rudder position and have the front blade barely glance off the front of the kayak between your knee and foot (if not miss the boat altogether!). The back blade should be completely in the water, as far towards the back of the boat as is comfortable, while your front hand crosses the

A Good Rudder: The Whole upper body is turned in an attempt to keep the line between the shoulders, parallel to the paddle shaft. The paddle is parallel to the direction of the kayak.

A Poor Rudder: Shoulders stay fairly square to the kayaks direction, causing the back arm to reach in a potentially dangerous position. This rudder's power will come from the small arm muscles, neglecting the larger back, chest and stomach muscles.

kayak, staying around shoulder level. Both your arms should be bent with elbows down, keeping your shoulders in a safe position. As with many comparable sports (skiing, snowboarding, surfing, etc...) your shoulders should face the direction you desire to go. This rule follows for surfing waves too, and we refer to it as the 'torso rotation' (see the segment on 'Torso Rotation') . In brief, torso rotation is the turning of

Keeping both arms bent, with elbows down, puts the shoulders in a safe position.

the shoulders that keeps the line between your paddle shaft and the line between your shoulders as close to parallel as possible! It is common for inexperienced surfers not to rotate their torso as it feels less stable at first than keeping the shoulders square with the kayak's direction. A rudder using the rotation of your upper body is much more effective, and usually causes your paddle to create less resistance with the water rushing by. On top of this, a good torso rotation will allow you to throw the wilder, more advanced moves!

——— *Let your kayak carve into turns by tilting it towards your rudder. When tilting your kayak, remember: keep your weight on a single butt cheek, not on your paddle.*

As your upper body goes through its motions, the lower body is doing its own thing. Your lower body is responsible for controlling the tilt of the kayak, and helping your rudder turn the boat. It's important to understand that the kayak and your legs aren't just along for the ride. Your kayak was designed to carve in the direction it's being tilted. Use this fact to help your rudder turn your boat. If you're carving back and forth quickly on a fast wave, or you're stuck in the trough of a wave, you might find that this technique of tilting your kayak into the

———————

Different kayaks carve to different degrees. Try out your kayak on an easy wave to see how much you can actually turn using only boat tilts. For the more dynamic waves, you may need to use the combination of a boat tilt and a rudder.

turns doesn't always work, and may result in a more efficient sinus flushing than a carve. For those faster waves, check out the following section.

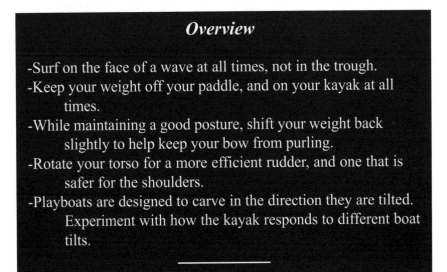

Overview

-Surf on the face of a wave at all times, not in the trough.
-Keep your weight off your paddle, and on your kayak at all times.
-While maintaining a good posture, shift your weight back slightly to help keep your bow from purling.
-Rotate your torso for a more efficient rudder, and one that is safer for the shoulders.
-Playboats are designed to carve in the direction they are tilted. Experiment with how the kayak responds to different boat tilts.

When Waves Get Steep and Quick

Every river has funky, fast and steep waves on it. These are the waves on which you can't just sit back and enjoy the sunset, but rather those on which you find yourself struggling to maintain control. Now that you're a confident front surfer, you have all the skills necessary to tear any wave to pieces! It's just a matter of practice, along with the consideration of a couple of new ideas.

The first thing to consider on steep, fast waves, is where to spend your surf time. The biggest problem on these waves is preventing your bow from purling. Staying out of the trough will most definitely help, but now, even the face of the wave can pose problems for your bow. There are two techniques that can provide the answers.

47

The first technique focuses on positioning your kayak so that its hull is not conforming to the shape of the wave. The only place you can do this is near the wave's peak. By positioning yourself here, you are balancing your kayak on a single point, which raises the bow. There is a fine line between surfing near the peak, and falling off the backside of a wave, so keep your weight upstream of the peak at all times. Doing this will

Balancing the kayak on the peak of a wave is a great way to prevent the bow from purling. It's a fine line between staying at the peak, and falling down the backside of the wave.

require small adjustments by shifting your upper body forward and backward. Your paddle also takes on a new role. Since you aren't relying on carving back and forth to maintain your kayak's position, an ideal turning rudder becomes less useful. Instead, use your paddle as a brake that will push you towards the peak of the wave, while gravity tries pulling you down the face. This braking stroke is done by pulling your front hand

A braking stroke in the process of being planted, to prevent the kayak from slipping further down the wave.

in front of your body while pushing the active blade further out to the side of the kayak. This exposes the back of your blade to the oncoming water.

The second technique that can be used to surf steep waves is a radical carving method. This technique involves ferrying back and forth across the face of the wave, exposing your bow to the current as little as possible. The key here is to spend the least amount of time pointing to 12 o'clock. Every additional microsecond that your kayak points to 12 is increasing the chances of your bow catching.

Since carving back and forth is once again a priority, revert to the safe rudder technique, making your kayak the most manoeuvrable. The major difference between this technique and the basic front surfing technique is the boat tilt that corresponds to your rudder. You'll now want to lean your kayak **away** from your rudder, ie. balance your weight on the butt cheek furthest from the rudder while establishing a steady tilt with your knees. The idea behind this is very simple. The tilt you are establishing

Keeping the bow from purling on a steep, breaking wave, by tilting the kayak away from the rudder. Notice the shoulders staying square to the main current, despite a 2 O'clock ferry angle on the kayak.

is the same tilt you hold when ferrying across a wave. The rudder is planted so that the kayak's bow won't get swept downstream. In this fashion, you'll be able to carve across the face of a steep wave holding a boat angle that can approach as much as 3 or 9 o'clock, while your shoulders stay square with the oncoming current. The next question is how does one turn and cut back in the other direction. Most waves have some type of shoulders. These shoulders are the best places to turn as they are usually a bit less steep than the center of the wave. As you reach the corner, your ruddering position has kept your body wound-up (see Torso Rotation for the wind-up). By digging

Start the turn as you reach the shoulder of the wave, by digging your rudder in deeply as a pivot from which to pull your bow around.

The stern slices under the peak of the wave, keeping the bow above the water.

As you reach 12 o'clock, change your boat tilt and the rudder you are using, to carve back across the face of the wave.

Ferry across the face of the wave to the other shoulder, and repeat the cutting back process.

your rudder in deeply as a momentary pivot, your body can unwind, pulling your legs and bow to 12 o'clock. By maintaining the same boat tilt (away from your paddle), you are essentially doing a low-angle stern squirt (see stern squirting). This forces your stern to slice under the peak of the wave, consequently pulling your bow upwards. Amazing! Once you've pulled your bow to 12 o'clock, change the rudder you are using and switch your boat tilt to start carving back in the direction which you came.

Overview

-Remember all the front surfing basics (safe rudder, separation of lower and upper body movements)

-Balance your kayak on the peak of the wave. Use a braking rudder and different body leans to hold your position.

or

-Cut aggressively across the wave's face.

-Tilt your kayak away from your rudder to hold a ferry angle.

-Turn by planting your rudder as a pivot. Unwind your body, pulling your legs square with your shoulders at 12 o'clock. Change your rudder and tilt at this point.

Recovery

No matter how good you get at front surfing, your bow will purl every once in a while. A great way of recovering from this is by quickly and briefly tilting your kayak on edge. The wide, flat top of your kayak catches a lot of water when it dives. When turned on edge, there is less surface area for the water to grab, and the bow's buoyancy can return it to the surface. With this technique, you'll soon be able to stay on a wave for as long as the pink Whip-It does!

Tilting the boat up on edge to relieve the water pressure that builds up when the bow purls. This tilt allows the bow's buoyancy to pop it back to the surface.

Side Surfing

*E*stablishing a balanced position in the trough of a hole, held perpendicular to the main current by the hole's recirculating water.

———————

Having the ability to confidently, and effortlessly, side surf a hole is essential to progress to the more advanced play moves. Why? This is because side surfing is a passive skill that relies completely on your balance. It will teach you to maintain a steady tilt on your boat while keeping your weight on your kayak, and off your paddle. This frees up your paddle to set up any number of other moves.

Entering the Hole

Entering a hole generally doesn't create the same problems for paddlers as getting out of a hole does. Still, it is worth mentioning a couple of the better ways to get established in a side surf.

The most controlled method of entering a hole is from an abutting eddy. Peel out of the eddy as you would for a normal eddy turn, and slide into the trough of the hole. Keep your weight over the kayak and on the downstream butt cheek, with your upstream knee lifting to help keep a steady downstream boat tilt. Your paddle should be held in a low brace position, ready in case it's needed. Aim to have your full kayak in the hole before your boat reaches a position perpendicular to the main current.

——— *Approach the hole as you would an eddy turn. Your speed and angle will be decided by the force of the current. The faster the water, the more speed and upstream angle you'll need.*

Slide into a side surf using the low brace position as a safety precaution. Don't unnecessarily lean on it.

The other reliable way of entering a hole is by dropping in from upstream. This can be a bit trickier as your downstream momentum comes to an abrupt stop, whereas peeling into the hole from an eddy never provides you with this momentum. When dropping into a hole sideways there are two components to consider: your kayak placement, and your body position. In terms of kayak placement, make sure that you hit a part of the hole that is powerful enough to stop you and your boat. Weak spots such as tongues are not strong enough to stop your momentum. This means you must really WANT to be in that hole. As for your body position, maintain good posture with a slight forward lean, balancing your weight on the downstream butt cheek and keeping a steady downstream boat tilt with your upstream knee. How much boat tilt you require will depend on the power of the hole, and the speed at which the current is taking you in. Your paddle should be held in a low brace position to prevent yourself from flipping downstream when you make contact with the hole (see The Braces). Though the low brace is the safest way to drop into a hole, protect your shoulders further by using your brace as little as possible on impact.

When dropping into a hole, sit up straight with a slight forward lean. Hold your paddle in a low brace position for the safest shock absorption.

Keep arms low, and head over the kayak when connecting with the hole.

The lack of volume in your playboat may cause you to wash right through a hole when dropping in. If you don't think the hole is powerful enough to completely stop you and your kayak, try dropping in with an upstream angle, almost as if you were attempting to front surf. Slow your momentum down with some forward strokes and lean back to keep your bow up as you near the hole. Once the hole hits you in the back, and stops your remaining downstream momentum, you can easily drop into a side surf. Keep some angle on your kayak as you enter the hole so that you can drop into your surf on a predetermined side.

Dropping into a weak hole: the body leans back to keep the bow up once the hole is reached, yet dropping into a side surf, the body moves forward into an aggressive, upright position.

Overview

-Choose a friendly hole to surf.
-Peel into the hole from an eddy using a low-brace turn, or drop in the hole from above with a low brace.
-Keep a steady downstream tilt on your kayak with your up-stream knee as you balance your weight on the down-stream butt cheek.
-Keep your paddle and arms low to protect your shoulders.
-If the hole isn't powerful enough to stop you, drop in with an upstream angle, while slowing yourself down with for ward strokes.

56

Hole Surfin'

With a bit of hole surfing practice, you will soon be able to relax and enjoy the ride with incredibly little effort. This is possible since surfing a hole is just a balancing act.

The ideal side surfing position is in the trough of a hole, away from any tongues that could make for a bumpy ride. Your weight should be balanced on your downstream butt cheek and completely off your paddle. Keeping your head over the downstream edge of the kayak will help to keep your weight where you want it to be. Meanwhile, it is vital that your upstream knee holds a steady downstream tilt on the kayak. This tilt should be enough to prevent your upstream edge from catching water, yet not a degree more. Any extra tilt on your kayak will provide for a bumpier ride, and make it harder to keep your balance. The trick to balancing your kayak this way is staying loose, letting your upper and lower bodies move independently.

Low brace side surfing position: the body's weight is balanced over the downstream edge, the boat is tilted just enough so the upstream edge doesn't catch water, and the paddle is held in an inactive low brace position, ready in case it is needed.

The high brace side surfing position: the paddle is held above the elbows, yet not above the eyes. The upstream elbow is kept close to the body to protect the shoulders and the downstream arm is not over-extended.

While side surfing, your paddle takes on a very passive role and should be held in a low or high brace position on the downstream side. When first getting comfortable with side surfing, you might find yourself spending a lot of time leaning or bracing on the paddle. Concentrate on moving that weight from your paddle to your butt. Your paddle is in the brace position in the event that you need it. It's not a crutch to lean on! By keeping all your weight on the kayak, your paddle is free to take strokes, and set up more advanced moves. Remember to take your strokes on the downstream side! A misplaced stroke on the upstream side while side surfing can result in a lightning-quick upstream roll.

By keeping all weight on the kayak, and off the paddle, the paddle is free to control the movements of the boat.

If you do manage to catch your edge and flip upstream, make sure to tuck both your body and paddle up to the kayak's deck. The upstream face of a hole isn't always deep, so tucking up can help you avoid any misadventures with rocks.

Advanced Side Surfing Tip

Sometimes, the hole you're intending to surf will surge or be so weak that it can't hold you in place. To prevent yourself from washing out of a hole, try rocking back and forth, alternately pushing your stern and bow back into the trough. A flat

58

hull will work even better in this situation as your ends will slide across the water, with ease.

Overview

-Balance your weight on your downstream butt cheek, keeping
it off your paddle.
-Tilt the kayak **just** enough to prevent the upstream edge
from catching.
-Hold your paddle in a low or high brace position, ready for
action if needed.
-Take all strokes on the downstream side of your kayak.

Escaping the Hole's Grasp

There are few situations that cause one to feel as helpless as getting stuck in a hole does. Unfortunately, most playboaters will at some point experience the isolation of being held in the trough of a powerful hole. Before you find yourself in this situation again, there are a few tricks to keep in the back of your mind.

The only place in a hole to exit in control is at its weak spots. These spots can be tongues, corners or even irregular, bubbly areas. The key is getting your kayak to these spots!

Digging deep into the foam pile with a back stroke, to grab the green water below. Notice the top hand staying in front of the body, keeping the shoulder in a safe position.

So, how do you move around in a hole? Well, you'll be happy to hear that it is surprisingly easy. The best way to escape a hole is simply to paddle out of it! In order to paddle out of the hole effectively, your weight will have to be on your kayak, and completely off your paddle. Your strokes must be on the downstream side of your kayak, and in order to be powerful, they'll have to be deep enough to catch the green water under the foam pile.

Sometimes the corners of a hole are too high or powerful to paddle easily out from. What may result is that you ride up the corner, high enough to see freedom, but get stuck, unmoving, while pulling on your paddle with all your might. As soon as you take your paddle out of the water for another stroke, Ssssslip.... right back into the jaws of the hole! In this case,

Building momentum by rocking back and forth from corner to corner, across the trough of the hole.

don't fight it! The water is going to win. Instead, let yourself slide back in, and even help the water out by paddling yourself further into the hole. The idea is to get a running start at the corner, building up enough forward momentum to break free. Ideally there will be another corner you can ride up on that will provide a further boost across the pit of the hole. If still you haven't built up enough momentum to escape the hole, at least you've moved further up the corner towards freedom. You can then shoot back deeper into the hole, or higher onto the other corner for a better run-up. Using this rocking technique, you should be able to break free of any reasonable sized hole.

There is a more advanced method of getting out of holes which wasn't available before kayaks had low-volume sterns and flat hulls. Take a forward sweep stroke with your kayak as flat to the water surface as possible, without catching your upstream edge. Keeping your boat flat like this allows it to spin in the trough of a hole. With the sweep stroke, pull your bow upstream (though not completely) using your whole upper body for power. The idea is to reach a blast position (facing upstream in a hole with the stern under the foam pile), as well as a ferry position. With this new position, the water is no longer

Pulling the kayak into a blast is a great way to build the necessary momentum to shoot out the side, or out a weak spot in a hole.

61

hitting the side of your kayak, pushing you only downstream. It is also now pushing you and your kayak perpendicular to the current like a regular ferry. By letting your blast drop back into a side surf, the current will grab your bow and forcefully swing it downstream. If you are at a weak spot in the hole, this swinging action can allow you to break free of the hole's grasp. You might even be able to shoot right out the side of a hole by ferrying across the trough in the blast position.

Overview

-Exit at a hole's corners or tongues.
-Keep your weight off the paddle so that you can take efficient strokes.
-Rock yourself back and forth across the trough of a hole in order to build up enough momentum to escape stickier holes.
-Pull your bow upstream into a blast position to ferry out the side of a hole, or to smash out a weak spot in the hole.

360's

*T*he 360 is the ultimate test of your ability to work with, and not against, the power of the river. It is also a great way to set yourself up for more advanced moves in a hole.

The best places to learn how to spin are at the weak spots of a hole. These are the tongues, or corners, where the green water visibly flows through. These corners should also feed some water back into the hole so that your spin doesn't pull you free of the hole's grasp.

To spin, you must balance your weight on the kayak, leaving your paddle free to control your movements. As discussed in the side surfing segment, this means keeping your weight on the downstream butt cheek at all times. Paddle yourself up a corner of the hole, letting your bow ride downstream until your kayak is parallel to the main current. Your head should be turned over your upstream shoulder allowing you to continually gauge your position relative to the seam of

Approach the spin corner slowly so as not to paddle all the way out of the hole.

The kayak has almost reached a point parallel to the main current. The head stays turned, looking over the upstream shoulder, eyes focused on the stern and the seam of the hole.

The kayak passes the direction of the main current. The boat is then tilted in the opposite direction as the head turns to look over the other shoulder. The other blade now controls the kayak's movements. Notice the slight forward lean throughout the spin.

the hole. The key is to reach a point high enough on a hole's corner to prevent your stern from catching, but without pulling yourself completely out of the hole. There is a fine line between the two, so approach the corner slowly to begin with in order to get a feel for the hole. If you feel yourself getting drawn back in and don't feel that you can complete the spin, don't fight the water. Keep a steady but strong downstream boat tilt, and let yourself slide back into the hole to try again. Eventually you'll reach a point where your boat stalls while pointing directly downstream, balanced and undecided on whether to continue downstream or to return to the hole. It is at this point that your spin progresses. Begin tilting your kayak in the opposite direction, and start controlling your kayak with your other paddle blade, on the new downstream side of your kayak. At this same time, turn your head to look over the new upstream shoulder, losing sight of the hole's seam and your stern for only a brief second. Keeping your weight forward through these motions will help prevent your stern from purling.

To continue with a full 360, repeat the same steps by back paddling up the corner of a hole. When you reach the point where your kayak is momentarily balanced, switch boat tilts and let your kayak slide back into the trough. Leaning slightly backward through this spin will help to keep your bow from purling.

Speed up the spin by actively forcing the downstream end between foam pile and the green water underneath.

As you might have guessed, there are more advanced techniques for the more difficult holes. If you are using a play-boat with low-volume ends, you'll find that you can speed up the spin by sliding the ends of your kayak between the pile and the green water underneath. If your kayak has a planing hull, you will find that you can flat spin in the hole as well. (see Flat Spinning)

Perhaps the most valuable advanced skill to perfect is reaching a balanced point at the top of a corner, and ferrying across the foam pile. This is especially useful in holes where the corners flush downstream rather than feed back into the trough. Following the standard spinning steps on a flushy corner will find you carving right off the wave. By ferrying across the foam pile towards the center of the hole, you can then turn, drop back in and resume your surf. This is also a fantastic way to set up the more advanced moves. A ferry such as this will mean a balancing act on aerated water, but is well worth practicing.

Ferrying across the foam pile, from a flushy corner towards the center of the hole.

Overview

-Spin at the hole's corners or tongues, letting the water do as much of the work as possible.

-Keep your weight on the kayak and off the paddle.

-Turn your head to look over the upstream shoulder, keeping your eyes on your stern and the seam of the hole.

-Pull yourself up the corner until you reach a balanced point in which your kayak is parallel to the main current, undecided whether to slide back into the hole, or continue downstream.

-Change your boat tilt, look over the opposite shoulder, and use the other blade for control as you pass being parallel to the main current.

-If the corner doesn't feed back into the hole, ferry across the top of the foam pile before dropping back in.

Enders

*L*etting the current take the bow or stern of your kayak underwater so that the boat's buoyancy can then shoot you vertically into the air.

Everywhere you look these days, it seems that someone is trying for the ultimate cartwheel ride. I must admit that it takes up a good portion of my paddling day. Every once in a while though, I'll straighten out my kayak, dive my bow underwater, and fly! There are few experiences that fully release the kid in me as a big ender does, and I'll always enjoy popping out of the water like a bar of soap from a wet hand.

Enders can be performed in all sorts of different places on a rapid, especially with the short boats of today. A successful ender is really only dependent on the water being deep enough, a good entry angle, and the acceptance of the possibility that you may land upside down.

Enders are easiest in a hole, but to ender off a wave from a front surf is more dramatic since the back of the wave drops away, providing that added feeling of air time. Wherever you might be endering, the critical steps are the same.

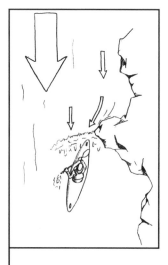

Keep the kayak pointed directly upstream relative to the current being entered, not to the main current.

It is absolutely essential to keep your boat pointed directly upstream. Any error here will transfer the energy necessary to send you air borne, into a quick flip and sinus douche. Keep your boat straight with a rudder on one side only. From this one side, by either pulling the back blade towards the kayak, or prying it away, you can make small adjustments to your kayak's angle, until you're shooting skywards. Once you're perfectly lined up, lean forward to engage your bow. As the bow dives underwater, transfer your weight onto your footpegs by standing up and leaning back. This backward lean will also help keep you from passing vertical and landing on your face. It can be tricky sometimes to engage your bow on a wave, especially if the wave isn't very steep. The most effective way to do this is to carve to the peak of the wave. Here, your bow will sit high out of the water. Lean forward and let your bow slide down the face of the wave and bury itself while holding the boat straight with a rudder. Engaging your bow in a hole can often be done without leaning forward at all. If you find your bow catching quickly, taking your kayak past vertical everytime, try leaning back sooner, or never leaning forward to begin with.

When endering from a wave, begin your approach at the wave's peak.

Stand up on your footpegs, lean back, and enjoy the flight!

Engage the bow, in the wave's trough, or further downstream, by leaning forward, and holding the kayak straight with a rudder.

Overview

-When engaging the bow: lean forward and keep your kayak pointed directly upstream with a rudder on one side.

-Stand up on your footpegs and lean back so your kayak doesn't pass vertical.

-When endering from a wave: begin at the peak, lean forward, and dive your bow, engaging it in the water before you move upstream of the trough.

Pirouettes

Spinning your kayak around on its end while performing an ender.

Almost ballet-like, a good pirouette will be smooth and seem effortless. Well, in actuality, it is a smooth and remarkably effortless move, and can be performed anywhere that you can get your kayak vertical. Once you have the knack of setting up your ender with a rudder on only one side of your kayak, you're well on your way to blowing your friends away with a full rotation.

There are two ways to effectively start your pirouette, and both methods begin after the initiation of a regular ender. The most reliable method is using a back sweep. As your bow dives underwater to start the ender, keep your kayak tiltless, and leave your rudder in the water to keep the kayak straight. When endering from a corner at the top of an eddy, this rudder is usually placed on the side of the main current. When you begin popping up, push forward with the back of your ruddering blade, against the current, and all the way to your

70

toes. As this lower hand sweeps forward, initiating the pirouette, your top hand and head will lead the kayak the rest of the way. The top hand punches across the boat in the spin direction (staying as low as possible to protect your shoulder), and your head turns this same way, trying to see around, and behind the

The Pirouette begins like a regular ender: forward lean to dive the bow underwater, rudder placed on the side the current is on, to hold the entry angle steady.

The pirouette reaches it's end! Keep those arms in tight and shoulders safe if you are flipping.

As the kayak begins to pop up, sweep the rudder all the way to the toes.

With the spin initiated with the sweep, follow through with your head and top hand leading the spins way.

kayak. If you land upside down, be careful that your top arm is not over-extended. If you do think you're going to land upside down, you're better off setting up for a roll in the air so that you can roll up immediately upon landing rather than landing on a big high brace, in an attempt to stay upright (unless of course, you truly enjoy the pain of a dislocated shoulder).

A more difficult method of pirouetting is the cross bow draw. This is a more advanced move as you leave your rudder, which is keeping you straight and balanced, and you commit your body to the move. Setting up for the cross bow draw is very similar to setting up for the standard roll. Once you have sunk your bow, and your boat has begun to pop back out of the water, reach with one blade to the opposite side of your kayak.

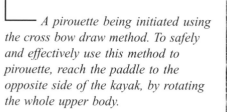
A pirouette being initiated using the cross bow draw method. To safely and effectively use this method to pirouette, reach the paddle to the opposite side of the kayak, by rotating the whole upper body.

Remember to rotate your whole upper torso when reaching across your bow. The further you rotate your torso to reach to the opposite side, the better. Grab as much water as possible and pull across your toes and the front of the kayak. This stroke initiates the pirouette, but it is once again up to your body and head to lead the way, pulling your kayak around with them.

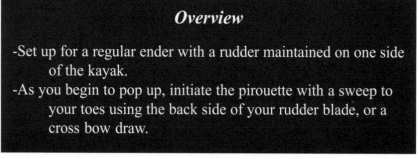

Overview

-Set up for a regular ender with a rudder maintained on one side of the kayak.
-As you begin to pop up, initiate the pirouette with a sweep to your toes using the back side of your rudder blade, or a cross bow draw.

-Follow through by pushing your top hand across the kayak in the spin direction, and turning your head the same way, trying to see behind the kayak.

-When cross bow drawing, reach to grab water with your blade on the opposite side of your kayak, rotating your whole upper body, while not over-extending your shoulders.

-If you find yourself flipping over, protect your shoulders and avoid landing on a high brace.

———————

Stern Squirting

Slicing the stern of the kayak underwater in a smooth arc to bring the bow vertically into the air. Usually performed when crossing eddy lines.

Stern squirting can be one of the best ways to improve your overall paddling, while at the same time leading you into some of the coolest, advanced moves. You'll develop a quicker roll, learn to separate your lower and upper body movements, and get more comfortable being vertical, yet maintaining control.

It must first be understood that getting vertical in a stern squirt does not mean that the correct technique is being used! With a powerful enough eddy line, even a big boat's bow can point to the sky. The correct stern squirt is still a very valuable move to learn, as it involves skills that are necessary for ALL advanced moves: cartwheels, flatspins, splats, etc... All are continuations of the basic skills required for a stern squirt.

Begin by practicing your squirts on a defined, deep, and not overly powerful eddy line. You SHOULD have trouble going vertical, but this way it is easy to break down the steps and find your weaknesses. Approach the eddy line as far upstream as possible, where there is a firm distinction between eddy and main current. This approach will have a major effect on the success of your squirt. Working back from the point of initiation, the ideal position to start your squirt is the moment your hip passes through the eddy line. At this point, your kayak

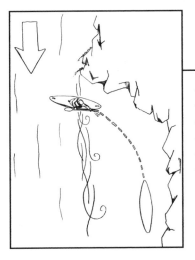

Begin the spin of the stern squirt before even crossing into the main current, with a smooth, arcing approach to the eddy line. Notice the kayak is perpendicular to the current as the hip breaks through into the main current.

should be perpendicular to the main current, with your bow continuing to turn downstream. Try to achieve this position without paddling overly hard at the eddy line, and also with a smooth, arcing line that begins deep in the eddy.

The ideal position to start the stern squirt: hip crossing the eddy line, kayak perpendicular to the current.

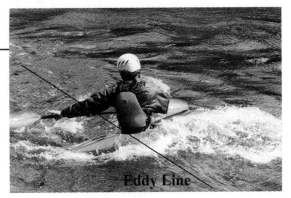

Squirting can be broken down into three separate skills: the paddle sweep, the torso rotation and the boat tilt. A successful squirt incorporates all of these at the same time.

A stern squirting sequence on flat water. Notice the arcing approach (fig 1.) and how the body stays ahead of the kayak's progression at all times.

Unlike making an eddy turn where you hold a comfortable downstream boat tilt, the idea is to sink the upstream edge of your kayak's stern. As you might have guessed, or learned, this is a committing move, that, when practiced, can result in a lot of river-bed scouting! Shift your weight to your upstream butt cheek, stabilizing an upstream boat tilt of <u>under</u> 20 degrees with your downstream knee. Don't over-tilt the kayak! As your balance, paddle sweep and torso rotation become stronger and more confident, you can get more aggressive with it. Make sure when you expose your upstream edge to the current that your body's weight is kept centered over the kayak. You'll find this requires some hip flexibility and a contraction of your stomach muscles on the downstream side.

Slicing the stern of the kayak underwater, while keeping the head and body balanced over the kayak.

Your paddle sweep and torso rotation go hand in hand and begin once the boat tilt is established. As your hips cross from eddy to main current, lean back to help force the stern of your kayak underwater. At the same time, rotate your whole upper body to face downstream, and reach as far to the stern of the kayak as possible with your paddle, without locking your arm at the elbow. (The further to the rear that your paddle starts, the more leverage your sweep will have). With the correct torso rotation, your paddle should be almost, if not completely, parallel to the kayak, as should your shoulders. The arm reaching back should be slightly bent, with the elbow down to protect your shoulder. The other arm stays tight to the body.

Stern squirt is initiated with a slight lean back, torso rotated, and back arm reaching back for the most leverage. Notice the head turned to watch the paddle placement. The turned head helps instigate the torso rotation.

With the whole blade in the water, sweep your back arm out and push it **away** from the kayak in a full arc. Though your back arm aggressively pushes your paddle to the side, the sweeping motion comes mostly from the unwinding of your torso. As your paddle sweep progresses, your blade should be fully under water. This will allow you to rotate your knuckles up, and push upwards with the back of your paddle against the water, as well as to the side. This upward push dramatically increases the power with which you may force the stern down, while also acting as an inverted brace. Meanwhile, following the

Having the paddle blade planted deeply underwater allows one to push up and out with the backside of the blade. This increases the power from which the bow can be pulled upwards.

paddle's sweep, your body moves to the bow so that you finish your stroke with a slight forward lean. This forward body motion can be confusing. You might ask why you'd want to put your body weight on the front deck if you're trying to raise the bow. Rather than placing your weight on the front deck, consider this pulling your legs upwards with your stomach muscles. You may find leaning back will get you vertical quickly and easily, but from this position you will have very little stability. This usually ends up with the kayak passing vertical or falling to one side. Keeping your weight forward is also key for more

Once you have sunk your stern underwater, it is crucial to level off the angle of your kayak at any time that your paddle is not actively spinning the boat. The reason is that unless the stern is being pulled downwards, the buoyancy of the kayak will pop the stern to the surface. This usually winds up sending the paddler for a drink.

As the bow is brought vertical, so is the body brought into a forward position. This position provides the maximum control, and is crucial for more advanced moves.

advanced moves, and if you can master it when stern squirting, you'll open up the doors to moves you've only dreamed about!

Overview

-Approach the eddy line with a smooth arc, initiating your stern when your hip passes the eddy line, and your kayak is perpendicular to the current.

-Tilt your kayak upstream (under 20 degrees) while keeping your weight centered on the kayak.

-Reach to the back of your kayak for the sweep, with full torso rotation and a slight lean back.

-Dig deeply with your sweep, pushing away from the kayak as your body unwinds. As the sweep progresses, rotate your knuckles up and pull upwards to increase your power.

-Bring your weight forward throughout the move, finishing in a forward, aggressive position.

Continuing Your Squirt

To continue your squirt, you must understand that your body leads the way, pulling the boat behind it. With that in mind, your body can only pull your legs around if it has a strongly planted paddle blade to pull from. Having said this, it is now reasonable to say that any time spent without a blade in the water is detrimental to your squirt. It is natural to follow the initial back sweep stroke, with a forward 'slap' stroke on the opposite side of the kayak, as it also acts as a brace. This stroke will help to push the stern further underwater, but is only effective very temporarily. The most efficient stroke to keep pulling the bow around and upwards, is a bow draw. The bow draw is essentially a duffek. This stroke involves reaching and rotating to the inside of the turn with both your paddle, and your body.

The stern squirt is initiated.

A 'slap' stroke follows the back sweep to continue the kayak's rotation.

A bow draw is planted with paddle shaft vertical for the most power. Notice the body leading the boat.

Your paddle blade reaches out to the side of the kayak, with the power face opened up to the bow of your boat. This stroke is most effective with the paddle shaft vertical (when looked at from the front), so cross your forehead with the top hand. Pull the blade forward in the water using the unwinding motion of your torso to do the work. When the blade has pulled its way to your bow, slice it back where it began, and start again. This can be a very powerful stroke, but if the top arm is held too high, or behind the head, it can also be very dangerous for your shoulder. Make sure to keep your hands in front of your shoulders at all times!

The Screw Up

The screw up is one of the most useful stern squirting skills to learn, as it gets used in all types of paddling. Most notably, you will use it when running rivers (to recover from unintentional or intentional stern squirts), or when trying vertical moves in a hole.

The idea behind the screw up is simple. When your stern squirt passes vertical, the screw up allows you to skip landing upside down, and roll with your bow still air borne.

Stern squirt is initiated with back sweep.

Forward 'slap' stroke brings the kayak vertical, and leaves paddle in roll set-up position.

Kayak passes vertical, and roll prepares to start.

Roll is performed as kayak continues to fall over.

Saved again!

Consider a standard stern squirt progression. The squirt was initiated with a back sweep, and continued with a forward 'slap' stroke, to get your kayak vertical. At this point, your paddle should be vertical, or almost vertical, alongside your kayak. Take a closer look. This is actually a perfect set-up position for the roll! As the bow passes vertical and begins dropping over the top of your body, begin your regular roll motions. Make sure not to over-extend your arms and put your shoulders at risk!

———————

Back Surfing

Using gravity to maintain a position on the face of a wave in which your kayak is facing downstream.

Perhaps we should call this the frustration surf! For many, back surfing is the most difficult move both to visualize and to perform. It is a skill that is worth investing the time to perfect though, as it will help a great deal when performing other advanced moves. After all, half of a cartwheel's time is spent with your bow facing downstream. So, how can one expect to have great control over the cartwheel without being comfortable in this position.

Getting Established on a Wave

Getting settled on a wave in a back surf can be your biggest challenge, but you do have three reliable options from which to choose. You can ferry onto a wave from an abutting eddy, drop onto a wave from upstream, or flat spin on the wave from a front surf to a back surf. The latter two methods are generally more difficult to do, so let's begin with ferrying onto a smooth wave with an abutting eddy.

Take into consideration everything that you would to establish a front surf on this same wave. How much angle and speed do I need? Where is the best spot to cross the eddy line?

——— Approach the wave close to the eddy line, with head turned towards the main current to see all river features.

└ Crossing the eddy line, the stern should go no further upstream than the trough of the wave. A sweep stroke in the main current helps to prevent the kayak from turning downstream.

Trough

Once you can visualize your approach, begin close to the eddy line. Build up some backward momentum with your head turned towards the main current so you can clearly see both the wave you are shooting for, and the eddy line that you must break through. Keep your eyes over this shoulder, with quick glances at your bow to ensure that your approach angle is accurate with the angle you visualized. Aim to break through the eddy line and onto the face of the wave with your stern no further upstream than the trough. A common problem when

---

Before you can consistently establish yourself in a back surf, you must first get truly comfortable with moving in a backward direction. Practice backward eddy turns and ferries, or even try running an easier rapid in reverse. Once you become comfortable paddling backward, you will be surprised how much your paddling improves in all sorts of different ways. On top of that, you have developed the skills necessary to back surf any wave!

The sweep stroke finishes maintaining the kayak's position on the face of the wave. The body's weight is balanced on the right butt cheek to maintain a steady downstream tilt

A rudder on the eddy side of the kayak prevents the paddler from carving right off the wave.

entering the current this way, is having the stern of your kayak carried downstream in a full eddy turn. This problem is worsened by breaking through the eddy line too far upstream (past the trough), or with too much downstream angle. So, adjust your approach accordingly. Even with a perfect approach, it can still be difficult to hold your ferry angle as you cross the eddy line. It will help to perform a back sweep in the main current, as you cross the eddy line. A forward lean at this time will help as well as it removes the weight from your stern, providing the current with less of your kayak to grab and force downstream. The sweep will hold your upstream angle for a moment, but it is important to finish off with a rudder on the eddy side of your kayak to fully establish control on the wave. It is also vital to maintain a steady downstream tilt on your kayak, as you would need for any ferry.

Another good method of establishing a back surf from an eddy is to approach the eddy line, slowly moving forward above the trough of the wave. The idea is not to cross the eddy line, but instead to let it spin you 180 degrees, or until you face downstream. Positioning yourself on the eddy line will move you further downstream towards the shoulder of the wave. Just

Approaching the eddy line slowly and above the trough of the wave, let the kayak spin to face downstream without crossing into the current.

As the kayak reaches the wave's shoulder, a sweep planted in the eddy pushes the stern into the current and on a ferry angle towards the far river-bank.

A second sweep is planted in the main current to maintain the ferry angle, while stopping any downstream momentum the kayak has picked up.

A rudder is placed in at the toes on the eddy side of the kayak to establish control on the face of the wave.

as you reach the shoulder, dig a strong back sweep into the eddy, pushing your stern into the current, and onto the face of the wave. It can be tricky keeping your stern from catching in the oncoming current. A forward lean, and a quickly established ferry angle towards the far river-bank (with the corresponding boat tilt) will certainly make this easier. Once the sweep has finished, leave that active blade in the water as a rudder to establish control, and to stop your kayak's turn from continuing.

Surf's Up... What now?

As the concepts behind back surfing are the same as those for front surfing, the rules to follow are the same as well. All your surf time should be spent on the face of the wave, and out of the trough. There are many reasons for surfing on the face, the most important ones being that the forces allowing you to surf are strongest here (see Standing Waves), and it is easiest to keep your stern from purling. There are a few different methods to hold your position on a wave and prevent your stern from purling, though some are better than others. The commonly seen method of lying one's body on the front deck of the kayak in prayer to the river gods, is not nearly as efficient a means as carving back and forth across the face of a wave. A braking rudder can also be used, though it is best saved for the steep, crazy waves. So, let's take a look at how to efficiently carve back and forth while back surfing.

Surfing on the face of a wave, relying on a good rudder and carves to keep the stern free of oncoming water, rather than a dramatic forward lean.

Carving back and forth across the face of a wave means keeping your kayak on a ferry angle at all times. The only time your kayak should be at 12 o'clock is for the brief instant it passes while in transition from one ferry direction to another. Any extra time spent pointing to 12 is increasing your stern's chances of purling. The control to do this will come directly from your rudder. Without a good rudder, your chances of both getting on a wave, and tearing it up once you're there, are much smaller.

A good rudder is positioned with your paddle held low to the water with one blade in at the toes, while the other hand is kept below shoulder level, and fairly tight to the body. The idea behind this rudder is to create as little resistance to the water as possible, so the closer to parallel your paddle stays to the length of the kayak, the better. Let's consider a situation where you

Your rudder is used for turning the kayak, not for leaning on. The blade should be held vertically in the water and placed at the toes to be most efficient. The other arm is held with elbow close to the body and hand below shoulder level, causing the paddle to lie almost parallel to the kayak's direction.

intend to carve to your right. Your rudder should be planted at your toes on the right side of the kayak with your left elbow held fairly close to your body. To do this comfortably, rotate your whole upper torso, keeping your paddle shaft as parallel as possible to your shoulders. The blade in the water should be vertical and not held flat to the surface of the water like a brace. When blindly surfing a wave, relying on all your senses to lead the way, it is a common error to lean on the paddle for comfort

---

The concepts behind back surfing are the same as those for front surfing, so practice front surfing the waves first. Get comfortable with the features of a wave, learning which parts are easiest to surf. If, when front surfing, one part of the wave continually causes your bow to purl, then count on having the same problem while back surfing! Look for landmarks on the peak of the wave so that when you are facing downstream, you can recognize your position.

as if it were a brace, or to reach forward with both arms as if you were pulling yourself through a large hole. Either of these techniques will result in lost control, and can pull you completely off a wave.

Carving back and forth across the face of a wave, using a well-placed rudder, and the carving capabilities of the kayak.

Once you're comfortable with the rudder, it's time to look at how the boat can help you carve up the waves. Playboats are designed to carve in the direction they are tilted, whether moving forward or backward. So get your kayak into the turning action by tilting it into your turns. If you're dealing with a steep and fast wave, this technique will probably land you upside down more often than not, and a more aggressive approach to carving will be needed.

Overview

-Stay on the face of the wave at all times, by carving back and forth, spending the least amount of time pointing towards 12 o'clock.
-Your weight stays on your kayak, not leaning on the paddle.

- When ruddering, get your paddle as parallel to the kayak as possible by rotating your upper torso to plant the rudder beside the kayak, at your toes. The other hand stays below shoulder level with the elbow held in close to the body.
- Remember that playboats are designed to carve in the direction they are tilted. Carve away!

Back Surfing the Crazy Waves

Back surfing the steep or quick waves requires quick reactions, since a slight misjudgment will usually mean the end of your surf. A good knowledge of the wave is crucial as well. Begin by front surfing the wave, learning its ins and outs so that you have a clear picture in your head of what your stern will be experiencing when back surfing.

Back surfing crazy waves poses the same major problem that front surfing does. How does one keep the upstream end from purling? Well, just as the problem is the same, so is the solution. There are two techniques to prevent your stern from purling. The first technique relies on balancing your kayak near, or at, the peak of the wave. The best way of doing this is with braking rudder strokes that grab the current which rushes by, pulling the paddler towards the peak of the wave. These braking strokes are done by pulling your rudder from the toes, to

The rudder pulled back from the toes to knee, grabs the water rushing by and pulls the kayak downstream, and up the face of the wave.

the knee, or even the hip.

Staying at the peak of a wave is a balancing act. Like any balancing act, small adjustments will be required to keep your weight in the right spot. When surfing near the peak of a wave, as long as your weight stays slightly upstream of the peak itself, your surf will continue. Keeping your weight where you want it will mean forward and backward leans. Don't be afraid to get your whole body into the act!

When balancing at the peak of a wave, shifting your body weight to the bow or stern can be useful for staying where you'd like to.

The other technique useful in preventing your stern from purling, is to carve aggressively across the face of a wave.

Aggressive carving means tilting your kayak away from your rudder instead of using its carving capabilities to help your rudder turn. The idea here is to maintain a ferry angle at all times, preventing your kayak from turning downstream with the use of a rudder.

Pull the stern around to carve in the other direction, using a combination of braking rudder, and aggressive carving. Notice the boat tilt away from the paddle. That enables the bow to slice under the peak of the wave, keeping the stern up.

With a firmly planted rudder and a very steep wave, you can even hold a ferry angle nearing 3 or 9 o'clock! The tilt on your kayak will usually decide the fate of your ferry. Like any ferry, your kayak must be tilted downstream, and like any tilt, the kayak must be put on edge with the body's weight staying over the top. The tilt once again comes from balancing your weight on the downstream butt cheek, while your upstream knee holds things steady.

Tilting the kayak away from the rudder.

Changing directions when surfing steep waves is a fairly simple skill once you've got the hang of leaning away from your rudder. To turn, dig your rudder deeply in the water. This blade has now become a pivot from which to pull your stern past 12 o'clock, and in the other direction. By keeping the same tilt on your kayak while doing this, your bow will be pulled under the peak of the wave, forcing your stern upwards. As soon as you pass 12 o'clock you then switch rudders and tilt your kayak in the other direction. The key is to spend as little time as possible with your stern pointing to 12 o'clock.

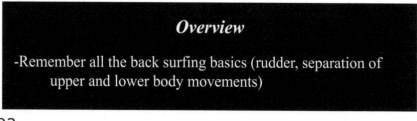

Overview

-Remember all the back surfing basics (rudder, separation of
    upper and lower body movements)

-Balance the kayak at, or near, the peak of the wave using a
    braking rudder and forward and backward leans to hold
    your position.
-Carve aggressively across the face of the wave.
    -Tilt your kayak downstream, and plant your rudder on
    the upstream side of the kayak to hold a ferry angle.
    -Change from one ferry angle to another with the mini-
    mum time spent pointing to 12 o'clock. Change by
    digging your rudder in the water deeply and pulling your
    legs back square with your shoulders. As you pass 12
    o'clock, change your rudder and boat tilt.

———————

Flat Spins

*U*sing a flat hull's planing capabilities to change your kayak's direction on the green part of a wave.

Without a doubt, the biggest evolutionary step for the playboat was the introduction of the flat-bottomed hull. When flat spinning became a reality, a whole new dimension of free-style kayaking opened up.

Before having a chance at spinning in control, you'll first have to be up to scratch with your front surfing. Are you comfortable carving back and forth across the face of a wave? What about your rudder? Is it at the back of the boat with your upper torso turned to keep your paddle shaft almost in line with your shoulders? If you've got this going, then prepare to throw some crazy spins.

Spinning from Front Surf to Back Surf

Initiating the flat spin is the toughest part, and when done right, everything else should fall into place. Using the steepest part of the wave, carve up high on its face or even onto the peak where your kayak will be the most manoeuvrable. If the wave is surging, wait until it grows to its steepest. The idea is to achieve some upstream momentum. As your bow dips, and you begin to drop back down the face of the wave, the time has come! Drop your back shoulder and engage your paddle

Starting high up the wave's face, the spin is initiated as the bow dips and begins to slide downward. The paddle plants deeply as a pivot, with the upper body rotated to keep paddle in line with shoulders.

behind the hip and slightly out to the side of the kayak, with your upper body wound up, keeping shoulders parallel to the paddle shaft. When this stroke digs in, push the stern of your kayak to the side and **away** from the blade, while at the same time unwinding your torso by pulling your legs around with your stomach muscles. Also at this time, shift your weight quickly to the bow. This weight transfer allows your stern to rise completely out of the green water, and skip effortlessly across the surface.

> The faster the water is rushing by the wave you surf, the higher your kayak will plane on the surface. The higher your kayak planes on the water, the more slippery it will feel, and the easier your boat will spin. These waves may not require you to pay as much attention to the finer technical points as it will seem you are surfing on ice. Slower waves will be the true test of your timing, weight transfers and stroke efficiency.

Carving high onto the face of the wave's steepest part.

The pivot stroke plants deeply on the inside of the spin. The stern is pushed away from it, while the legs pull the bow towards it.

As the legs are pulled to the pivot blade, the paddler's weight is transferred to the bow of the kayak, allowing the stern to skip across the water. Notice how flat the hull stays to the water surface.

The spin completed, you'll notice the pivot blade has maintained its position in the water throughout the move. It now acts as a rudder to control the back surf.

While going through these motions, there is one other thing to consider. Very simply, the flatter you keep the hull of your kayak relative to the surface of the water, the easier the spin. The whole idea of not putting a strong downstream tilt on your boat will be a frightening thought to begin with, but it is imperative in order for you and your kayak to skip across the water. The only way to keep your hull this flat to the water is to let your hips be loose and flexible, moving independently from your upper body. As long as your weight stays over the center of the kayak, you'll be amazed at how little downstream lean is needed.

Overview

-Initiate the spin the moment you begin to gain upstream momentum, dropping from high on the face of the wave, downwards.

-Start the spin with your torso wound up, and by dropping your shoulder to engage a pivoting stroke behind the hip and slightly out to the side of the kayak. As you push the stern of your kayak out to the side and **away** from the paddle, unwind your body (pull your legs around) using your stomach muscles.

-Quickly transfer your weight from stern to bow, allowing the stern to rise and skip freely across the water.

-Keep your hull as flat to the surface of the water as possible.

Spinning Back to a Front Surf

Spinning from a back surf to a front surf is a bit more difficult only because you don't have as much visual help while facing downstream. Otherwise, the motions are very similar. Initiate the spin high on the face of a wave (or at the peak) the moment you feel yourself gaining upstream momentum (as you begin to drop down the face). Rotate your head and torso in the

—— *The spin is initiated with a pivot stroke planted deeply at the toes, while head and torso are rotated in the direction of the spin. This happens just as the kayak begins to slide down the face of the wave.*

direction you wish to spin, if your rudder hasn't already done this to your body naturally. Drop your front shoulder, and dig in the paddle blade deeply at your toes. Consider this blade a pivot from which to push your bow out to the side and away, while pulling your bow around by use of your stomach muscles. Another important movement when the pivot stroke bites into the water is your weight transfer from the bow to the stern of the kayak. Removing the weight from the bow allows it

— *Starting from high on the wave, head and torso rotate in the spin direction, as paddle gets planted deeply in the water as a pivot.*

— *With pivot blade planted, and head and torso leading the way, the stomach muscles pull the bow around.*

— *Body weight is transferred to the stern, allowing the bow to rise and skip across the water. Note the flatness of the hull to the water.*

— *Spin finishes with pivot blade maintaining its position throughout the move. It now acts as a rudder to establish control in a front surf.*

to skip across the surface of the water effortlessly. Don't forget that your hull **must** remain as flat as possible to the water. If you find yourself carving off the wave, your hull probably wasn't lying flat enough, or perhaps your weight wasn't removed completely from the bow.

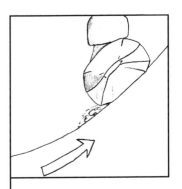

— Keeping the hull of the kayak flat to the water surface allows the boat to sit higher in the water, as the paddler's weight is distributed over a wider area.

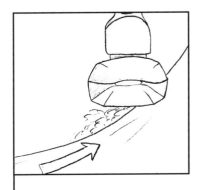

— Keeping the hull of a kayak level, but not necessarily flat to the water surface, may cause an edge to dig in. The boat will then carve rather than slide.

Overview

-Initiate the spin as you start to gain upstream momentum, dropping from high on the face of the wave, downwards.

-Lead the spin with your head and upper body.

-Transfer your weight from the bow to the stern, enabling the bow to skip effortlessly across the water.

-With your shoulders turned in the spin direction, drop your front shoulder, and deeply dig your paddle at the toes. Consider the blade in the water a pivot from which to push the bow to the side and away, while your legs pull it around.

-Keep the hull of your kayak as flat to the surface of the water as possible.

Full 360's

A full 360 can be done by putting together the two halves already covered. This will work on many of the fast and steep waves where it feels as though you're surfing on ice. There is a more efficient, and quicker method of spinning on these waves though, which will also make 360's possible on other, smaller waves as well. This method focuses on blending the two halves together without pause. Leading the spin with your head and body becomes all the more important for this 360, as does keeping your boat flat and making sure your strokes are all deeply planted.

360 is initiated like a regular flat spin.

As soon as first stroke finishes, the next stroke is planted by simply dropping the shoulder and blade in the water. Head and body continue to lead the way, pulling the bow around by use of the stomach muscles.

After digging in your first blade and starting the spin, you establish a lot of spinning momentum. The only way to keep this momentum going is by planting a second stroke as quickly as possible, from which your stomach muscles can keep pulling the bow around. This second stroke is placed by immediately dropping your shoulder on that side, and planting the blade between knee and hip, rather than all the way up at your toes. Remember that your stomach can only pull the kayak around while there is a blade in the water for it to work with. This is why getting your second stroke in quickly is more important than taking the extra time to reach all the way to your toes for a more powerful stroke. Your 360 is now one fluid motion!

With deep and powerful paddle plants, an aggressive unwinding of the body, good body weight transfer, and a flat hull against the water, you might find that you don't even need a second stroke to complete the 360!

Overview

-Keep the initial spinning momentum going with a second stroke placed as quickly as possible, between knee and hip.
-Keep the boat flat to the water surface.
-Lead the whole spin with your head and upper body.

Cartwheels

An advanced move performed in a hole, in which the bow and stern rotate around the body, staying 45 degrees or more past horizontal.

The cartwheel is the most impressive trick to watch a kayaker perform as no other move requires the paddler to maintain a comparable level of control while toying with the river's awesome power. This is probably why it has become the ultimate goal for so many playboaters.

So how do you do a cartwheel? That's a very difficult question to answer. Obviously, every hole is quite different, and only practice can teach you what techniques work better in each situation. Luckily though, there are some basic principles that apply to all cartwheels.

A large misconception about the cartwheel is its resemblance to an ender. Unlike when doing enders, where both kayak and paddler get thrown into the air, when doing cart wheels, the paddler ideally remains in a fixed spot, acting as the axis, while the boat rotates around him like the wheel. Think about the cartwheel as an elevated flat spin, because this is in fact what it is! Consequently, many of the steps and skills required for flat spinning are used for cartwheeling as well.

For simplicity's sake, let's consider a deep, friendly hole for the following skills.

Set-up

A good set-up is vital for any cartwheel's success. The idea is to establish control on the hole's foam pile so you can initiate the bow of the kayak in the best spot, with the desired angle and with as little upstream momentum as possible. Getting onto the top of the foam pile from the trough of the hole is a bit of a trick in itself. The only reliable method of doing this is by paddling your kayak up a corner or tongue in the hole, then ferrying across the hole's boil line. Once balanced on the foam pile, alternating braking strokes (small back strokes around your hip) will provide you with the control necessary to keep

Alternating braking strokes planted around the hip will pull the bow of the kayak back and forth, while slowing down any upstream momentum.

from sliding back into the trough. The reason for balancing like so, is that any upstream momentum you possess when initiating a cartwheel will dive you deeper into the green water. This will pop you uncontrollably into the air, and downstream of the hole. Your braking strokes are also very useful for setting up the correct boat angle with which you must initiate the bow.

Initiating

The initiation of your cartwheel is heavily dependent on
your set-up. With a poor set-up, a successful initiation will be
difficult. Similarly, a poor initiation makes the continuation of
your cartwheel sequence very difficult.

The whole idea when initiating your cartwheel is to use as
little green water as possible to get the spins going. This really
means that it is preferable to use as little of the river's power as
possible, relying on your body's power instead. The further
downstream on the foam pile you attempt to initiate, the less
green water your bow can grab, and the more your own
strength will be required to engage the bow. By aiming to
initiate your bow at the seam of the hole, you're usually using a
good balance of the river's and your own strength. As for the

*With your paddle planted
firmly and deeply in the water
as a brake (to stop or greatly
slow down any upstream
momentum) a good spot to
initiate your bow is at the seam
of the hole.*

angle your kayak should enter the water, that will vary with the verticality of the cartwheel you're setting up. Regardless of what this angle is, it should stay consistent throughout that one move. Considering a left-side cartwheel (kayak tilted to your left side), your set-up should be around 1 o'clock. As you attempt to initiate, pull the bow around to at least 12 o'clock. What this does is establish some spinning momentum before the move has even begun. If you are hoping to do fully vertical ends (end referring to each of the elevated 180 degree spins), then bring your bow down to enter the water at 12 o'clock. In this case, your kayak should be almost completely on edge so

—— Setting up with a 1 o'clock angle. Notice the braking rudder in the water, preventing the kayak from building any upstream momentum.

—— Having chosen an entry point, the braking rudder digs in deeply, pulling the kayak's bow around and downwards. The kayak's tilt is being set at this same time.

—— The bow enters the water at the seam of the hole, having being pulled from a 1 o'clock angle past 12 o'clock, and still moving towards 11. The tilt on the kayak is around 45 degrees. With plenty of spinning momentum built up at this point, and a 45 degree tilt on the kayak, we can expect a low-angle cartwheel.

A low angle cartwheel, as expected from the set-up and initiation.

that your kayak slices downward with minimal resistance. If you're shooting for an easier to control, low-angle cartwheel, then set up again at 1 o'clock, and aim to break the water with your bow past 12 o'clock, closer to 11 o'clock. In this case, your kayak should be on edge closer to 45 degrees. The low-angle cartwheel is a better move to practice as you will maintain more control of your kayak throughout the move. If you managed a good 1 o'clock set-up before initiating at 11, then your kayak will have had the chance to build plenty of spin momentum. This momentum will make your cartwheel easier to control.

Winding Up The Bow

As mentioned earlier in the initiation segment, the more you rely on your body power to initiate the cartwheel, the better. The reason for this is that when you rely on the power of the green water (rushing into and under a hole) to take your bow and start your cartwheel motion, the less certain you can be of the result. If you physically throw your bow down in a certain direction, with a certain tilt on the kayak, you'll have a much better idea of what will happen. This is where winding up the bow comes into play.

The idea behind winding up the bow, is to lift your bow into the air in order to have some extra energy available to throw the bow downward. To make your bow rise, you'll have to do three things simultaneously: hold your kayak steeply on edge, perform a forward sweep, and shift your weight back slightly in order to help sink the stern.

The stern of the kayak is sunk and the bow pulled into the air using a forward sweep and the stomach muscles.

Most of the body's weight stays on the extreme edge of the kayak. Keeping the head upright will help to keep too much weight from falling on your paddle. Also, notice the stroke pulling around a foot to the side of the hip.

Now that you can wind up your bow, you've realized that keeping it there is impossible! This means that if you want to use the maximum amount of the gained potential energy, there can be no hesitation before smashing your bow downward.

As the forward sweep turns to a back sweep, the torso rotates to face the water, and the legs are pulled aggressively down. To become comfortable with the initiation of your bow and your stern, practice rocking them alternately into the air.

To throw your bow down, turn your forward sweep into a back sweep using the non-power face of your blade. As this blade digs into the water, shift your weight to the front of the kayak, and aggressively rotate your torso downward to face the water. From this position, your legs get pulled down by your stomach muscles.

Winding up the bow like this is best practiced on flatwater, but you'd be surprised how often it can be used in whitewater to initiate the cartwheel. In small pourovers, you may require the full wind-up, but in other holes, you may need just a touch of this wind-up power. You may need such a small amount, that it won't be noticeable to spectators. Regardless of how much you use it, remember to aim your bow wisely, and with a sensible boat tilt for the type of cartwheel you are attempting.

———————————

Whether you need to use a bow wind-up to initiate the cartwheel, or not, you'll still need to pull your bow downward, which will use many of the same motions.

The first thing to remember when cartwheeling is that your body weight must stay over the kayak, as it does for spins. The moment your weight falls onto your paddle, your kayak is at the mercy of the river gods! The paddle actually takes on a lesser role than many people expect. It is used mainly to establish a pivot and a brace in the water, as well as a brake to prevent your kayak from gaining upstream momentum, and diving too deeply in the green water.

The paddle digs deeply into the green water below the pile. This blade is acting mainly to prevent further upstream momentum, and as a pivot from which the stomach muscles can pull the bow downward.

Plant your paddle out to the side of the kayak and beside your hips, deep enough under the foam pile to grab the green water rushing by below the pile. Dropping the shoulder that is on the same side as this blade helps get your blade deep, and also forces your torso to turn into this stroke. Hold your top hand firmly, around shoulder height, and about one foot in front of your chest. Do not let this hand cross the invisible line that splits your body into two equal halves! Both of your arms should stay bent for protection, while your shoulders stay parallel to the paddle shaft, as always. This shoulder position is very important when cartwheeling as once again, your power will be coming from your whole torso rather than just your

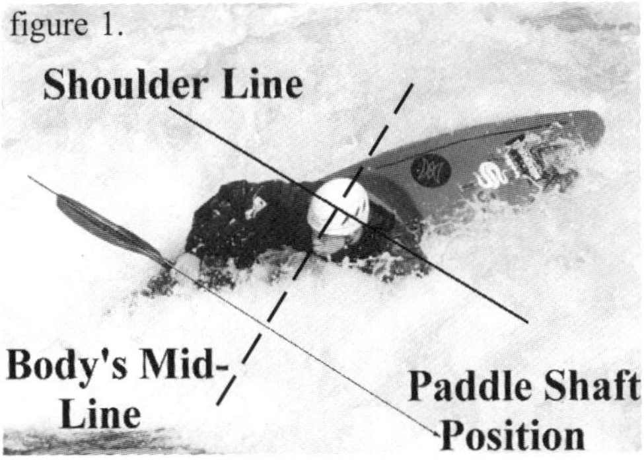

figure 1.

Shoulder Line

Body's Mid- Line

Paddle Shaft Position

Initiating the bow
Things to notice:
1. Paddle shaft parallel to shoulder line.
2. Front hand staying well away from the body's midline.
3. Body weight is slightly forward to help force the bow downward.
4. Torso rotated into the spin, leading the kayak.

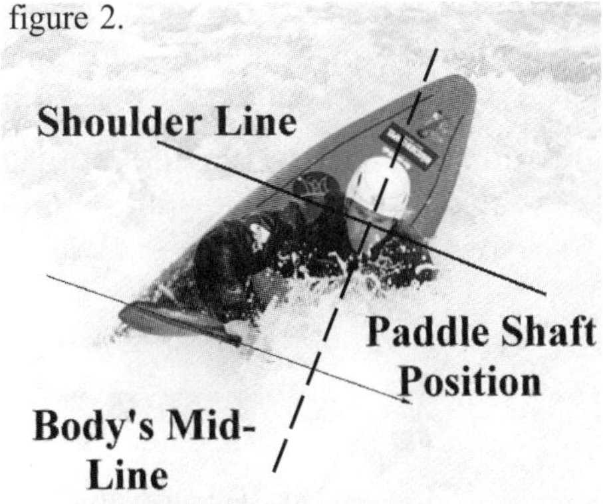

Immediately after bow initiation
Things to Notice:
1. Paddle shaft kept parallel to shoulder line.
2. Front hand continues to stay well away from the body's mid-line.
3. Leaning back slightly as body weight is transferred to the foot-pegs.
4. Torso rotated to stay ahead of the kayak's progression.

figure 2.

Shoulder Line

Paddle Shaft Position

Body's Mid- Line

Comparing the front arm position in the two photos, we see very little change relative to the upper body. This is a good indication that the body power needed for the cartwheel comes from the stomach muscles, more than anywhere else.

arms. As you push down on your firmly planted pivot blade, it's up to your stomach to pull the bow down at the hole's seam, towards the blade that is in the water. This motion is sometimes referred to as 'closing the scissors'. Keep a **slight** forward lean to help force the bow down with your body weight. As your bow engages, it is vital that you keep your eyes on the seam of the hole, and don't turn your head downstream. Your head has a tendency to turn your upper body with it. Put the two together, and you will probably find yourself doing a pirouette.

——— *Eyes are kept on the seam of the hole allowing the paddler to know their position in the hole at all times, while preventing the cartwheel from turning into a pirouette.*

Once the bow has begun to move downward, shift your weight from your butt onto your feet, pushing on your footpegs while leaning back ever so slightly (see figure 2.). Pushing down on your footpegs can help to get your bow to pass underneath you. If you find your bow is passing underneath you just fine without your weight on the footpegs, then you are probably diving your bow too deeply in the green water.

Initiating From Your Stern

Initiating the stern of your kayak is another option that has both its strengths, and its weaknesses. The only reason this move is more difficult is because you must do the work by feel as much as by sight. On the other hand, initiating the stern should be easier as your pivot stroke is planted at the knee and pulled on, rather than planted at the hip and pushed on. We can achieve more power from this pulling action than we can from the pushing action used when initiating the bow. Just look at a rower. A rower has his or her back to the direction of motion, so that all strokes are pulled!

Keep in mind those same important ideas that are needed to initiate your bow, and apply them to the stern. Firstly, it is important to know your position in the hole at all times so that you can initiate your stern at the seam of the hole. So, turn your head upstream, in the direction you plan to spin. Secondly, you want to establish some spinning momentum before engaging the stern in the water. This momentum is established by a good set-up angle pointing to the opposite side of 12 o'clock than the side that you'll be initiating on. (ie. Set-up at 11 o'clock, initiate stern past 12 o'clock, towards 1.) The angle of tilt on your

—— Eyes are kept on the seam of the hole, as the stern is initiated. Spinning momentum is built up as the stern is pulled from 1 o'clock past 12 o'clock, and with a boat tilt of around 45 degrees, a low-angle, controlled cartwheel can be expected.

—— As expected, a low-angle cartwheel is initiated The deeply planted pivot/brake stroke remains at the knee, allowing the stomach muscles to continue pulling the bow around.

kayak as it enters the water is completely dependent on where your stern is initiated. Should you be attempting a vertical cartwheel, your stern will enter the water at 12 o'clock while being tilted almost completely on edge. For the preferable, low-angle cartwheel, you may need only a 45 degree tilt on your kayak as your stern is pulled past 12 o'clock before it enters the water.

Your paddle is once again going to take on the role of a pivot, (from which the bow is pulled around with your stomach muscles) and a brake (to slow any upstream momentum). This pivot/brake stroke is planted at your knee, deeply enough to catch the green water below the pile. Leaning ever so slightly backward will help you initiate the stern, though you **should** be able to do so from an upright position. Once your stern has initiated, pull your body forward into a more aggressive and stable position, which sets you up for any subsequent ends (remember stern squirting?).

As the stern is initiated, the body leans forward. This is a more aggressive and stable position from which to control the kayak.

Initiating a cartwheel is both a powerful and graceful move in which different techniques will work in different holes. As long as the water is deep, don't be afraid to experiment! If you are new to a hole, it's not a bad idea to sit back and watch how the best paddlers are getting their kayaks vertical.

Overview

-Aim to engage your bow or stern at the seam of the hole, with as little upstream momentum as possible, and with some spinning momentum already achieved from your set-up.
-Keep your weight on your kayak, and not on your paddle.
-Drop your shoulder to deeply plant a pivot/brake stroke in the green water under the foam pile. Your top hand stays at shoulder level, around a foot in front of its shoulder, and **never** crossing the body's mid-line.

-When initiating the stern the pivot stroke is planted at the knees.
-When initiating the bow, the pivot stroke is planted at the hip.
-As you push or pull on your pivot stroke, pull the bow around with your stomach muscles.
-Keep your eyes on the seam of the hole **at all times**.

Linking Ends

So you've initiated the bow and are getting vertical, but are having trouble continuing your cartwheel sequence. Congratulations! You've learned the toughest part of the cartwheel. Now, only practice will make perfect, since the better your initiation becomes, the easier it will be to get that next end. When practicing, keep in mind that good, **quick** paddle placements are crucial for getting multiple ends.

The initial stroke has reached a point where it is no longer effective.

The shoulder drops to engage the next stroke at the knee, deep enough to grab the green water below the pile.

Once your bow has been pulled to your pivot blade to the point where your paddle is no longer useful, quickly move to your next stroke. This following stroke is planted deeply around your knee, by simply dropping the upstream shoulder. Placing this second stroke at your knee won't provide you with as much leverage as reaching to your toes will, but it is **more** important to have a blade planted quickly and firmly in the green water, than it is to take the extra time to reach to your toes. The reason for this is that having a blade in the water allows your stomach to pull the kayak around continuously, keeping the spinning momentum going. When your paddle is out of the water, the river can begin to take more control of your kayak's movements. These movements aren't as predictable as those that you control with your paddle in the water. A last thing to consider

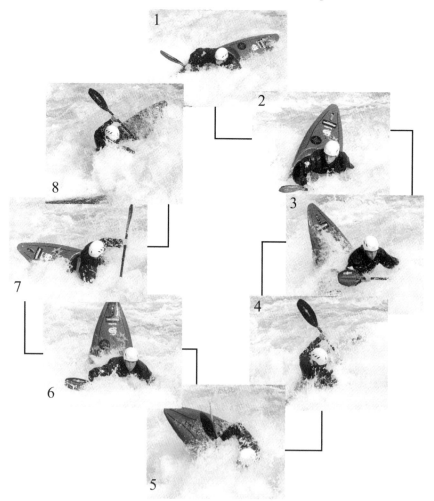

with this second stroke, is the turning of your head. As soon as this stroke is planted, your head turns to look over your other shoulder, leading the kayak, while attempting to see the seam of the hole once again.

As the second stroke is planted, the head turns leading the kayak in the spin direction.

Now let's look at the following stroke, needed to smash your bow downward once again. As with the last stroke, speed is of the essence. As your bow passes vertical and drops back down towards the seam, rotate your shoulders to face downward while pulling your legs behind you. Using the backside of your paddle blade, reach deeply at the hip to grab the green water below. From this pivot stroke, the whole sequence will repeat itself.

As the bow drops towards the seam, the shoulders rotate to face downward, staying ahead of the kayak. Notice the paddle blade planting in the green water.

Cartwheels involve spending half your time facing downstream. It takes practice to become comfortable with having your back to the oncoming water. Spend some time paddling backwards in more controlled conditions. Try doing some reverse eddy turns, back ferries, or back surfing. The more comfortable you become moving backwards, the more possibilities will open up for radical play moves.

Cartwheeling is one of the most difficult freestyle moves for a reason. It involves the use of all major playboating skills, from your upper torso rotation, to keeping your head and weight centered over the kayak. It will take awhile to co-ordinate all the necessary motions, but as long as you have a clear picture in your head of what it should look like, practice CAN make perfect! So, next time you're at the local play spot, think about the key points mentioned here, and take a good look at someone who is putting them into action.

Overview

-Once a stroke is no longer being actively used to spin the kayak, move as quickly as possible to plant the following stroke.

-By keeping your shoulders ahead of the kayak's spinning progression, each stroke planted becomes a pivot from which your stomach muscles can pull the bow around.

-Lean slighlty forward when the bow is air-borne, while leaning slightly back when the stern is in the air. This puts you in a stable and aggressive position, prepared for the follow-ing end.

-Keep your eyes on the seam of the hole at all times. When your bow spins downstream, turn your head at the same time as you plant your next stroke.

Splitwheels

Pirouetting your kayak 180 degrees while cartwheeling, in order to change the direction of your cartwheels.

I remember watching my first split wheel a number of years ago, and being completely amazed. Here I was figuring out how to get the third end of a cartwheel sequence, and this fellow (whom I soon had to compete against) was pirouetting

180 degrees while continuing to cartwheel! It seemed to demonstrate the ultimate in control. Back on the water a couple of hours later, I was frustrated with trying for the big cartwheel sequence, and decided to give the 'splitwheel' a whirl. In a matter of minutes, I was splitting away, making myself appear much better than I really was. The moral here is that the splitwheel is a very impressive manoeuvre to watch, but is a remarkably simple variation of the cartwheel. If you can cartwheel, you can splitwheel! You just have to be willing to try something new.

Learning the splitwheel is by far easiest when tried immediately after initiating your first end. Considering a cartwheel with body facing to the left, your first paddle stroke will be the braking/pivot stroke at your left hip. In a typical cartwheel, this first stroke is followed quickly by a second stroke, placed at the knee on the right side of the kayak. When splitwheeling, instead of moving to this second stroke, your first blade remains in the water through the whole move. As your bow is initiated, instead of keeping your eyes on the seam of the hole, let your head turn downstream. Your kayak tends to spin in the direction your head turns, so this will start to pirouette your kayak. Pushing with the backside of your pivot stroke, across the bow of your kayak, and pulling your right knee upwards will carry the

To pirouette the kayak, the pivot blade draws across the bow while the right knee pulls upwards. This kayak has almost pirouetted to the point where the hull faces directly upstream.

pirouette through. Now it's a matter of stopping the pirouette before you've spun too far. To stop the pirouette, simply stop drawing your blade across the bow, and more importantly, turn your head back in the direction that it came. This should stall your pirouette quite effectively. Aim to stop the pirouette with the hull of your kayak facing directly upstream. Continue to pull your right knee up, until the kayak is right on the edge that was initiated to begin with. Once your kayak is on this edge, you can continue with the regular cartwheeling technique. Plant your paddle at your knees as a pivot, deep enough to reach the green water below the pile. Leading with your head looking back upstream at the seam of the hole, pull the stern down and your bow up.

The Splitwheel

Overview

-Practice the splitwheel after initiating the first end of a cartwheel.
-The blade that you initiate your bow with is the active blade
   and should be kept in the water throughout the whole
   move.
-After initiating the bow, start pirouetting your kayak by turning
   your head downstream, drawing water with the backside
   of your pivot blade across your feet, and pulling up your
   upstream knee.
-Stop the pirouette once your hull is facing upstream. To stop
   the pirouette, stop drawing your blade across the bow,
   and turn your head back in the direction that it came.
-Continue pulling up your upstream knee until your kayak
   is on edge once again.
-With kayak on edge, and head turned upstream to look at the
   seam of the hole, plant your blade in the water at
   the knees and continue with the regular cartwheel technique.

Playing Around

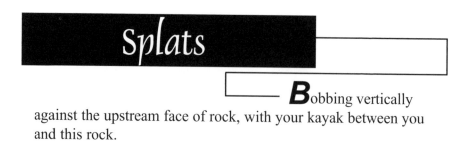

Splats

Bobbing vertically against the upstream face of rock, with your kayak between you and this rock.

Another move developed through squirt boating is the splat. Not too long ago, splatting was a move tried only by the bravest paddlers in glass squirt boats. But, with the development of today's little boats, splatting has become popular

among a much wider audience. Not only are the short boats relatively easy to get vertical, but being made of tough plastics, they are a lot more forgiving when playing around (or on) rocks. It's easy to see that splatting is catching on with paddlers these days, as it gets harder to find a rock that isn't decorated with multicoloured plastic shreds.

To splat a rock, you first have to recognize a good splat rock. A good splat rock is one with a smooth upstream face, which the current runs into, creating a pillow. The current hitting this rock should be deep, and not overly powerful. Rocks are best avoided if they are undercut in any way, or if the current leading away from the rock is not deep enough to roll.

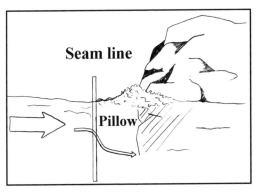

Anatomy of a pillow
The pillow is the area of relatively still water that is piled against the upstream face of a rock. The seam line is the point at which the main current meets the pillow, and is forced around to the sides of the rock.

As you approach the rock, you have two choices from which to initiate the splat. You can either squirt your bow into the air, or you can take a much more aggressive approach and ride up the rock to get vertical. If you don't like leaving large chunks of your kayak behind, then stick to the squirt approach. Regardless of what you choose, you'll be relying on the rock's pillow of water to keep you bobbing vertically.

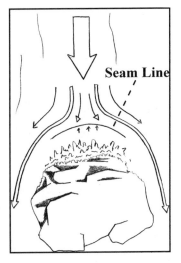

Top view of a splat rock and it's pillow. The seam line will have the look of a well-defined eddy line.

First, let's look at the squirt approach. Since you have already read the stern squirting section hundreds of times, and have practiced your squirts for hours on end, we don't need to go into specifics on your technique. Just remember to keep your weight forward in the kayak once your bow is airborne, otherwise you could easily continue past vertical when splatting. The only vital aspect of your approach is keeping your kayak between you and the rock. Otherwise, there is no single way to set up a splat. With an eddy abutting the splat rock, it will usually be easiest to squirt as you cross the eddy line. If there is no eddy, then you may have to float sideways towards the rock, initiating your stern squirt as you reach the seam. Pillows provide at least two very different currents as water bounces off the rock, forming a wall (or pillow) of still water into which the main current

Approaching the rock from upstream by floating sideways. Eyes are spotting the seam line to know when to initiate the stern squirt.

When the seam line is reached, the stern squirt is initiated with a back sweep on the downstream side of the kayak.

Once the bow is in the air, the body moves forward as it does in a normal stern squirt. This stablilizes your splat, and helps prevent your kayak from continuing past vertical.

continuously runs. This makes for an incredibly powerful and distinct seam line. As you sink your stern, bringing your bow to face downstream, the main current will help push you vertical, while the pillow will do the same from the other side. With both these forces working towards the same goal, the toughest part of the splat may be to stall your squirt so that you don't pass vertical and land upside down! The only way to avoid this is to change where you initiate the squirt, and to keep your weight further to the front of your kayak.

The other option that plastic playboats provide, is to attack the rock more aggressively. Approach the rock at around an 11 or 1 o'clock angle. When you hit the pillow, take a big sweep stroke on the side needed to turn the boat to 12 o'clock, lifting your bow as high onto the rock as possible. Lift your bow by tilting your kayak into the sweep, and shifting your weight slightly to the back of the boat to sink the stern. Once your bow is up, get your weight forward in the kayak. Definitely not a move for kayak polishers!

Starting from 11 o'clock, a powerful sweep stroke, and a slight lean back sinks the stern, while pulling the bow upwards, and to 12 o'clock.

Notice how far forward the body is leaning. With the bow touching the rock, and the main current still hitting the stern, staying forward like this is the only reasonable way to keep from passing vertical. It also will allow you to initiate other moves such as splatwheels.

Overview

-Recognize a good splat rock (one that isn't undercut, and is deep upstream as well as on the sides)

-Using your <u>perfected</u> squirt technique, approach the rock sideways and squirt your stern underwater at the seam line, keeping your kayak between you and rock.

-Approach the rock at an 11 or 1 o'clock angle. With a sweep stroke, bring the bow to 12 o'clock and as high onto the rock as possible. Help sink the stern by leaning back and tilting your kayak into the sweep.

-Lean forward when your bow is up to prevent yourself from continuing past vertical.

Bow Splats

Splatting a rock with your bow down and stern in the air.

Initiating a bow splat is not an easy move to do, and will generally take a very small boat, a very powerful pillow, and/or a very strong paddler.

Approach the rock perpendicular to the main current. When you reach the pillow, wind up your bow (see winding up your bow in the cartwheel segment) and throw it down at the seam line. Obviously, you'll be doing this with your kayak tilted

As the splat rock is approached, the bow is wound up, to be thrown down at the seam line.

126

away from the rock - unless you're trying a face splat! Your wind-up must be very aggressive to bring the bow completely under your body, but remember that the pillow is going to help push your kayak vertical. This means that you don't need to throw your bow down vertically, but can slice it down at an angle closer to 45 degrees. Whatever the angle at which you

— Shoulders are rotated downwards, as the bow is pulled aggressively through the water by use of the stomach muscles

— As the bow slices underwater further, the body weight is transferred onto the foot pegs. Using a low brace the kayak is helped to balance in this position.

throw the bow down, the important thing is to get your weight onto your foot pegs as quickly as possible. Once there, lean slightly backward, while using the back side of your paddle blades to low brace. Only practice in this position will let you keep yourself balanced.

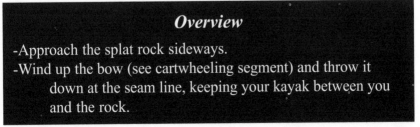

Overview

-Approach the splat rock sideways.
-Wind up the bow (see cartwheeling segment) and throw it
      down at the seam line, keeping your kayak between you
      and the rock.

Splatwheels

Cartwheels performed in the pillow along the upstream face of a rock, while keeping your kayak between you and that rock.

Splat wheels are a lot like regular cartwheels. The main difference is that you set up your splatwheel from a stationary, vertical position. This means a serious body commitment will be needed to get the cartwheel going, but otherwise, it's business as usual. Start by getting vertical in either a bow or stern splat. Let's consider that a bow splat was initiated, placing your stern in the air. Let your stern begin to drop in the opposite direction from where it came. As it drops, turn your head and upper body right around in the spin direction, staying ahead of your

After winding up the bow, the splatwheel begins as the bow is thrown downward aggressively at the seam line.

From the pivot blade, the kayak is pushed past vertical, keeping the spinning momentum going.

As the stern drops downward, the head and torso rotate in the spin direction, and the paddle prepares to plant its next pivot stroke.

kayak. From this rotated position, plant your paddle firmly in the water and out to the side of your kayak at the knees. As with regular cartwheels, consider the blade planted as a pivot from which to pull your bow around in pursuit of your upper body. Leaning back slightly as the stern drops to the water surface will help provide the stern with an added bit of momentum. As the stern breaks through the water surface though, get your body forward quickly so that you don't pass vertical. With

—— As the pivot stroke plants deeply, the head leads the way.

—— With body forward, keeping the body's weight over the kayak, the bow is pulled past vertical to keep the spinning momentum going.

your weight now forward, keep your bow moving through the air until it passes vertical and begins dropping down towards the water on the other side. By turning your upper body and head to face the water, you have arrived in the position that initiated your bow in the first place. Now, you have the momentum of your bow falling from a vertical position rather than from just your wind-up. These steps can be repeated as long as you stay balanced over your kayak!

The splatwheel is a fun move to try, and an impressive move to watch, but as with anytime you play around rocks, elbow pads would not be a bad idea!

Overview

-Once the initial splat is initiated, attempt to keep the spin
  momentum going.
-As an end drops, rotate your upper body and head to stay
  ahead of the kayak.
-Plant your paddle deeply and out to the side of the kayak as a
  pivot from which to pull your bow around with your
  whole upper body.

———————

Rock 360's

A full spin done while balanced on a rock with the ends of your kayak out of the water.

If you don't mind hacking up your kayak a bit, then the Rock 360 is one of the best ways to spice up runs, or sections of a river that you no longer find quite as challenging. Remarkably, the Rock 360 is a combination of some basic skills you've been over a number of times already. Imagine that!

For this move to be possible, you first have to find a safe, flat, rock that can balance your kayak on a single point and that otherwise won't impede your boat from spinning. Running up onto this rock and stopping long enough to get your spin going is the next step. This balancing act is a trick in itself to perform, and can only be done consistently with a lot of practice. Like

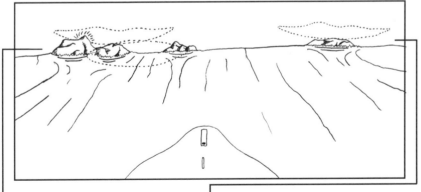

These rocks do not enable the ends of the kayak to spin unimpeded. There is also the possibility of broaching should the paddler slip back into the current sideways.

This rock allows the kayak to spin freely, and has no close by rocks that could cause both ends of the kayak to pin simultaneously.

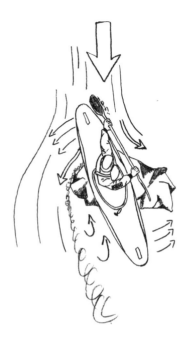

many aspects of kayaking, your approach angle and last stroke will decide your rock stalling fate. Approach the rock from directly upstream, in the line that hits your target most directly. With your approach decided, rather than simply bombing towards the rock at full speed, use controlled strokes, focusing on your last one to pull you onto the rock. Keep in mind that it IS best to err on the aggressive side, causing you to bounce over and past the rock, instead of getting pinned on the upstream side of the rock.

Once balanced on the rock, rotate the entire upper body and reach to the stern for a back sweep. The paddle plants as a pivot from which the body can unwind, pulling legs and the kayak around in a spin. Notice the back of the blade exposed to the current, providing the added power of the moving water to initiate the spin.

Spin your kayak in the direction that allows the water to help. This usually means that if you ride up onto a rock on the left bank, you'll probably want to spin your bow to the left. Start your spin as your last stroke lifts you on top of the rock, and your stern clears the water upstream. The spin is initiated with a stroke similar to that used to begin the stern squirt, the only difference being that you must keep your weight centered over the length of the kayak. Wind up your body by rotating your torso in the direction you are going to spin, then plant your paddle at the stern of the kayak. With this stroke planted, it's then a simple matter of doing a back sweep while unwinding your torso. Ideally, this stroke is planted so that the back of your paddle blade grabs the water that rushes by the rock,

132

With paddle firmly planted, the legs continue to pull the kayak around as the upper body pushes the paddle away from the stern in a wide arc.

adding its power to your stroke and providing you with an incredible amount of pull. Once your kayak is spinning, you generally won't need to use such radical strokes to keep the spin going. So, rather than fully extending your arms to plant the next stroke, get your next stroke in the water as quickly as possible by dropping the shoulder on the side of the blade being planted, and digging that blade in at the knees. As always, lead the way with your head, keeping your upper body ahead of the kayak's progression. Before you know it, you'll be working on your Rock 720!

Overview

-Run up on a rock that is both safe, and won't impede the spinning of your kayak.

-Spin in the direction that will allow the water to help (if you grab water moving by the right side of the rock, you'll spin left)

-Once your stern clears the water upstream, initiate the spin by winding up your upper body as you reach your paddle to the stern, then unwinding with a back sweep.

-Your successive strokes require less energy and rotation. Rather than reaching for a powerful stroke, get your paddle in the water as quickly as possible to continue pulling your legs around with your upper body.

Flatwater Cartwheels

Cartwheels performed without the help of a hole and its strong current. The power needed for the flatwater cartwheel comes almost exclusively from your ability to wind up both boat and body to aggressively throw down the ends.

Five years ago, who would have believed that we'd be doing flatwater cartwheels in plastic boats? These are squirt boat moves. Right? The fact is, most of today's freestyle moves have evolved directly from squirt boating! Let's look at cartwheels from a plastic boater's perspective!

What makes a cartwheel more difficult on flatwater than in a hole, is having to throw down the kayak's volume into non-aerated water, without the help of the hole's dynamics to pull your ends through. The only way to get around this problem is with good technique, and sheer force!

By this point, you should already have the skills needed to make this happen. You've learned to use the rotation of your torso to harness the power of the biggest muscle groups, you've learned how to lead moves with your head, and you've learned how to wind up your bow.

A strong bow wind-up is crucial to the success of the flatwater cartwheel.

Notice how much the shoulders have rotated ahead of the kayak. This massive upper body wind-up will be necessary to pull the bow down with enough force to slice through the non-aerated water.

Begin by paddling forward and picking up a bit of speed. This forward momentum helps you get your weight onto the foot pegs once you've initiated your bow. Remember the wind-up. The idea is to lift your bow as high out of the water as possible in order to achieve more energy to slice your bow downward. To do this, you'll have to do three things simultaneously: put your kayak right up on its edge, perform a forward sweep to pull the bow upward, and shift your weight slightly back to help sink the stern. The idea here is to force the stern underwater as much as possible so that the bow will rise.

Now that you can rock your bow up into the air, you've realized that keeping it there is impossible! This means, if you want the maximum amount of energy to smash your bow into the water, there can be no hesitation before following through with the next step. What the next step entails is throwing the bow of the kayak underwater as deeply as possible, while getting your body weight on your foot pegs. To do this, rotate your upper body and head downward to face the water, and plant the paddle blade that performed the forward sweep at your hip and about a foot to the side of your boat. Just like a normal cartwheel, your front hand stays shoulder height, and in front of your body. As you push down on your blade, you provide a pivot from which your stomach muscles can pull your legs aggressively downward. You'll encounter a lot of water resistance, so getting your weight onto the footpegs will be the only way to force your bow to keep going down. As the bow is driven underwater, it will help to use your paddle to push your weight up and onto the footpegs. The closer to vertical you can get your kayak in this method, the better. When your kayak is vertical, you will have more potential energy to throw the following end down.

Your pivot blade allows your legs to pull the bow downwards, but also can help push the body onto the footpegs.

As the stern passes vertical, a slight lean back will increase the momentum of the stern as it drops to the water.

Once you've reached vertical, keep your spinning momentum going by attempting to engage your next end right away. Let your stern pass vertical and drop back to the water, keeping the same angle on your kayak. Shift your weight back, and plant a powerful pivot stroke at your toes. It is once again crucial that your upper body and head rotate ahead of the kayak so that your stomach muscles can continue to pull your bow around in pursuit. As the stern slices underwater, bring your body weight forward, in a balanced, aggressive position.

With shoulders and head leading the way, the cartwheel sequence continues.

The body stays forward, balancing the kayak, and preparing for the following end.

Similarly, when going for your third end, keep as much momentum as you can. As your bow passes vertical and falls towards the water, keep your weight forward, turn your upper body aggressively ahead of the spin, and dig the pivot stroke in, out to the side of your hip.

The body begins to rotate in order to beat the bow to the water.

Flatwater cartwheels are **very** aggressive manoeuvres that will take about all the strength you can muster. Even so, it takes a small kayak relative to a paddler's size for this move to be possible. A small paddler in a big boat, or a bigger paddler in a bigger boat, may not physically be able to perform these cartwheels. If this is the case, don't worry; the world's not working against you! Though you might not be able to throw flatwater cartwheels, the added volume of your kayak can be to your advantage in other situations.

Overview

-Start with a bit of forward speed.
-Wind up your bow aggressively to achieve enough momentum to slice your bow underwater. As your bow dives deeply, push and throw your weight onto the footpegs.
-As your kayak reaches vertical, don't stop, but keep the spin momentum going.
-Initiate the stern with your weight shifted back, your head and torso rotated to lead the way, and a strong pivot blade planted out to the side of your kayak, at the knee.
-As your bow slices upwards, bring your weight forward to balance the kayak, and prepare for the following end.

An air-borne cartwheel performed while launching off the peak of a standing wave.

First impressions are everything. Right? Well, if you want to make a lasting first impression, then enter a play area with a full rotation... Air-borne! This is what an airwheel is. By building up some downstream speed, and initiating a cartwheel as you hit the peak of a wave, you can achieve an almost fully air-borne cartwheel!

Learning to fly like this can be remarkably easy if you're comfortable with the basics of the cartwheel. Going back to the basics, what have you learned? You've learned to lead the spin with your upper body rotated ahead, pulling the bow of the kayak around by use of your stomach muscles, and a firmly planted and powerful pivot blade. Nothing changes here! The only difference with an airwheel is that you are forcing your bow through air rather than water. The key then is in building up the initial momentum for the rotation.

Approach the standing wave you'll launch from with some speed. There is no need to paddle like mad, but having some forward momentum will help you take off, and make your airwheel all the more dramatic. As you reach the peak of the wave, follow the motions for winding up your bow (covered in the cartwheel segment). Tilt your kayak right up on its side, keeping your weight over the very edge of it, and take a for-

A launching forward stroke gives the kayak a boost off the peak of the wave.

Head and shoulders turn to face the water while a firm pivot stroke is planted high on the face of the wave.

ward stroke. When winding up the bow, this stroke was used to pull the bow as high as possible. When taking this stroke during an airwheel attempt, there is no need to pull your bow so high. Why do you not need to wind up your bow as high as possible? As you ride up the face of the wave, your bow is already pointing slightly upwards. Also, when you pass the peak of the wave and smash your bow downward, your kayak will have further to go to reach the water, as the backside of the wave drops away. This gives you ample time to build spinning momentum without having to fully wind up your bow. Use this forward stroke instead to help launch yourself off the wave. With this in mind, your forward stroke will take place as you ride up the face of

— As the bow is pulled aggressively downwards using the stomach muscles, the body is thrown downstream, and over the top of the kayak.

— To continue the wheel, lead with your head and shoulders, planting a deep pivot stroke from which to pull the bow around.

the wave. Once this launching stroke has been taken, plant a deep, pivot stroke at your hip, while rotating your shoulders and head to face the water. With a strongly planted pivot stroke, and your torso rotated in the spin direction, you can pull the bow downward quickly and aggressively with your stomach muscles (like a normal cartwheel!) As the bow is driven downward, it is vital that you push off the wave with the backside of your pivot blade, and throw your weight downstream and over the top of the bow. Aim to establish your weight on your down

Staying balanced on your kayak, continue as you would with a regular cartwheel. Notice the head leading, and the body in a forward position.

stream footpeg. With practice, the bow smashing downward, and the body being thrown downstream should easily provide you with enough momentum to carry your stern all the way through the wheel. If you have maintained your balance over the kayak at this point, you can even continue the sequence as you would performing a normal cartwheel (rotating your upper body and head ahead of the kayak, and planting the next pivot stroke).

Overview

-Approach a standing wave straight on, with some forward speed.

-Perform the wind-up motions as you ride up the face of the wave, but instead of pulling your bow up high, use the forward stroke to launch off the peak of the wave.

-Plant a pivot stroke deeply at your hip, high on the face of the wave.

-Turn your head and shoulder downwards, pulling your bow aggressively down in behind.

-Throw your weight downstream and over the top of the kayak.

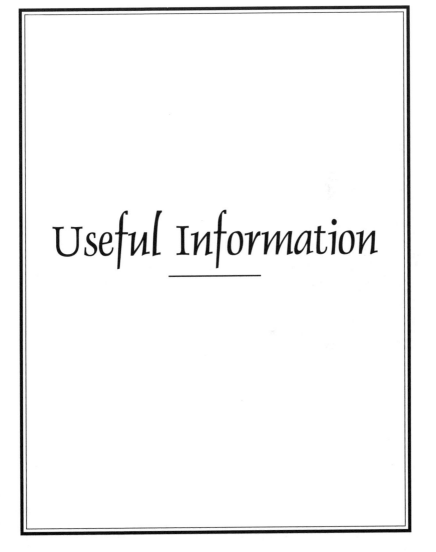

Useful Information

Glossary of Terms

Airwheel - An air-borne cartwheel performed while launching off the peak of a standing wave.

Backside (of a wave) - the part of a wave downstream of the peak, where water flows downhill.

Back surfing - using gravity to maintain a position on the face of a wave in which your kayak is facing downstream.

Blast - front surfing in the trough of a hole, with your stern under the foam pile.

Boat tilt - the leaning of your kayak to one side, while your weight stays over the kayak.

Body wind-up - The rotation of your upper body in the direction you wish to turn your kayak.

Boil line - The point on a hole's foam pile in which the water on the upstream side flows upstream, while the water on the downstream side flows downstream.

Bow - the front end of your kayak.

Bow wind-up - The pulling of your bow into the air, in order to achieve more energy with which to throw it downwards.

Brake - a stroke planted when surfing, to slow your upstream momentum.

Cartwheel - An advanced move performed in a hole, in which the bow and stern rotate around the body, staying 45 degrees or more past horizontal.

Corner - the side of a hole that can be used for spinning, setting up advanced moves, or exiting.

Cross bow draw - a stroke planted to initiate a pirouette, with your front arm completely crossing the bow of the kayak.

Deck - the top of your kayak.

Downstream - The direction in which water is flowing.

Eddy line - the line of turbulent water separating two currents that are traveling in different directions.

144

Ender - letting the current take the bow or stern of your kayak underwater so that the boat's buoyancy can then shoot you vertically into the air.

Face (of a wave)- the part of a wave upstream of the peak and downstream of the trough, in which water is flowing uphill.

Ferry angle - The angle of a kayak to the current that allows the water to push the kayak laterally.

Flat spin - Using a flat hull's planing capabilities to change your kayak's direction on the green part of a wave.

Foam pile - the aerated, recirculating water that forms the white part of a hole.

Front surf - using gravity to maintain an upstream-facing position on the face of a standing wave.

Green water - the non-aerated water that flows into and under a hole.

High brace - a method of preventing a flip using the power face of your paddle on the water.

Holes (hydraulics) - a type of wave in which the water piles up on itself, forcing aerated water back upstream and into the trough.

Hull - the bottom of your kayak.

Low brace - a method of preventing a flip using the back side of your paddle on the water.

Off-set - the angle at which a paddle's blades are twisted rela tive to each other.

Peak - the highest point on a wave.

Pillow - The area of relatively still water that is piled against the upstream face of a rock.

Pirouette - spinning a kayak around on its end while performing an ender.

Planing hull - A flat hull that, when surfing, will rise to the surface and slide like a car on ice.

Purling - the action of one of your kayak's ends burying into the oncoming water when surfing.

Rock 360 - A full spin done while balanced on a rock with the ends of your kayak out of the water.

Rudder - a blade that is planted in the water when surfing to control the direction of your kayak.

Screw up - a roll performed when passing vertical in a stern squirt, that uprights the kayak before your bow touches the water.

Seam (of a hole) - the point in the trough of a hole at which the foam pile meets the green water.

Seam (of a pillow) - The line dividing the current that flows into the rock from upstream and the rock's pillow.

Shoulder (of a wave) - the sides of a wave (usually present where a wave borders an eddy).

Side surfing - Establishing a balanced position in the trough of a hole, held perpendicular to the main current by the hole's recirculating water.

Slap stroke - a forward stroke used when stern squirting to maintain balance and push bow further into the air.

Splat - Bobbing vertically against the upstream face of a rock, with your kayak between you and this rock.

Splatwheel - Cartwheels performed in the pillow along the upstream face of a rock, while keeping your kayak between you and that rock.

Splitwheel - Pirouetting your kayak 180 degrees while cartwheeling in order to change the direction of your cartwheels.

Stern - the back end of your kayak.

Stern squirt - slicing the stern of the kayak underwater in a smooth arc to bring the bow vertically into the air. Usually performed when crossing eddy lines.

Surge - a fluctuation in the size of a water feature.

Sweep - a stroke used to turn your kayak.

The 360 - changing the direction of a side surf by riding up and spinning at the weak spots in a hole (tongues, corners)

Tongue - a weak spot in a hole that water flows through freely.

Torso rotation - the turning of your upper body that gets all major muscles involved in your strokes.

Trough - the lowest point on a wave.

Upstream - The direction from which water is flowing.

Advertisers

rock solid

Aqua-Bound Technology Ltd

USA 1160 Yew Avenue, Blaine, WA 98230
CANADA Unit 1, 9520-192nd Street, Surrey, British Columbia V4N 3R7
New address as of Dec 1998 19077-95A Ave, Surrey, British Columbia V4N 4P3
Tel: (604) 882-2052   **Fax:** (604) 882-9988
E-mail: sales@aquabound.com   **Website:** www.aquabound.com

1997 Worlds Rodeo Champion Kayak
Men's K-1
Women's K-1

perception
one with the water

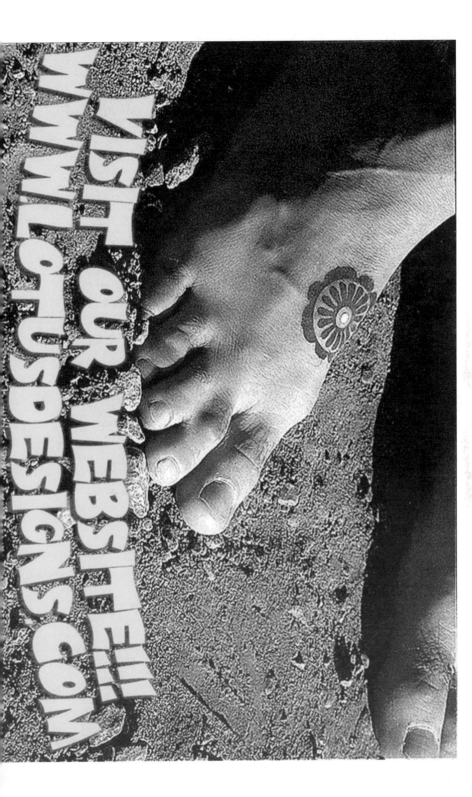

Pyranhas patrol
these waters...

Necky

1100 Riverside Rd, Abbotsford, B.C V2S 7P1 Canada
P O Box 1206, Sumas, Wa, 98295, U.S.A

This is an advertisement for Wilderness Tours.

Wilderness Tours

School of Kayaking Big Rapids, Warm Water All Summer

ON THE WORLD FAMOUS
OTTAWA RIVER

160,000 cfs spring flood levels
45,000 cfs summer. Always
great paddling on the Ottawa

Learn the latest playboating
moves and the most
advanced basic skills from
some of the world's most
accomplished paddlers.

Five day all inclusive and
weekend kayak packages for
beginners to expert.

Featuring
Top instructors Eric Jackson,
Kevin Varette, Tyler Curtis
Jamie Simon and others

WT

1-800-267-9166
www.wildernesstours.com
email: wt@wildernesstours.com
Box 89, Beachburg, ON Canada K0J 1C0

Enjoy our full service Outdoor Centre Resort and unsurpassed
hospitality. Paddle all day and relax in wilderness luxury.
Featuring: camping. chalets.cedar cabins.luxury log cabin. volleyball.
hot tubs. bungee jumping. fireside lounges evening entertainment and
much more. Call and book your paddling vacation on the Ottawa

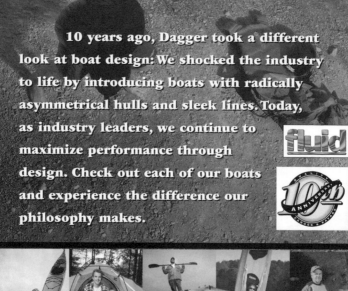

For photo credits, paddlers, and locations write or call
Wave Sport P.O. Box 775207 Steamboat Springs, CO 80477
Phone: (970) 736-0080 www.wavesport.com

Grateful Heads™

MIND BLOWING GRAPHICS

KEVLAR® REINFORCED PLASTIC

MANY DIFFERENT STYLES

6-WAY ADJUSTABLE HEAD-LOCK
STRAPPING SYSTEM

FULL COVERAGE INTERCHANGEABLE
MINI CELL FOAM LINERS

STAINLESS STEEL RIVETS

TRIM THAT WON'T COME OFF

WE BACK UP OUR WORK
LIFETIME
WARRANTY

John Lovett shootin' in Westwater Canyon, UT
Christie Dobson designin' in Chattanooga, TN

Grateful Heads™
Extreme *Quality* for Extreme FUN!
555 Green Gables Rd
Friendsville, MD 21531
301.746.4015 **phone**
301.746.4012 **fax**
grateful@gcnet.net **e-mail**
www.GratefulHeads.com **web**

KEVLAR® HELMETS
Kevlar® is a DuPont registered trademark.